FAITH AND FATE

Faith and Fate

Emily Thorne

To order additional copies of this book, contact:
Xlibris LLC
1-888-795-4274
www.Xlibris.com
Orders@Xlibris.com
587964

I would like to dedicate my book to my partner Sam
and my mum Joan who always stood by me.

Early Life

It all began in the midseventies on a cold midnight of February. My mother already had two children, one of which she had also given up for adoption just like she was going to do with me. Only five days after I was born, she decided that she didn't need me and that the easy escape for her was to give me away for adoption too, just the way she did with my sister before me. I stayed in the hospital until the age of two and discovered later on in life that this was also the hospital where my mother's sister worked at the time of my birth. My first recollections of myself are in a children's home in Pliska from the age of two until seven. I was the only colored child at that time and quickly started to understand the racial differences between me and others.

Most of the children avoided me because of my skin color apart from only one person. She became my best friend later; her name was Emma. She was the same age as me, and we would both be sent to the same boarding school. We would do almost everything together. She had her disadvantage of being overweight and I being coloured, so I guess we needed each other as friends to overcome the challenges ahead in an orphanage where cruelty had no mercy if you were weak. She, unlike myself, had parents who would visit her from time to time and for some unobvious reason to me back then was left in social care and only later found out that she had a sister. Her parents were so poor that they were surviving on people's kindness. From my time in the children's home, I was hoping to have had my mother visit me too. The need to have her in my life was growing inside me every day in the cold relationship I was receiving from the staff and other children.

I was dreaming that she would come looking for me one day, that she will have regrets for leaving me for adoption. With nostalgia, some days I would wait by the front gate hoping to see her among the hundreds of people passing by and trying to imagine how she would look. Sometimes I would put my hand through the hole in the gate, trying to catch with the grasp of my fingers the passing skirts of women and get their attention. Sometimes some would stop and smile with sympathy and others would make faces of disapproval at my actions, and yet my search of my mother would continue. Other days I would be playing in the yard and if not with the others then by myself, climbing the cherry tree that not many were brave enough to climb at my age; I would hide there for as long as I felt right, far away from everybody in my own world of dreams. I have to say I did like to have my privacy from a very early age, and so when there was an opportunity, I was up there in the tree, watching the street, and each time someone came in and out the gate, I hoped that one of them would be my mother. Some of the teachers must have noticed my weird behavior from time to time and often ignored me, I suppose, to avoid dealing with me.

Some afternoons we were all taken out for a walk, which was often followed by treats. Sometimes I would be left in the orphanage with an excuse that my clothes were dirty and for no other reason. Some teachers were very easygoing and made me feel comfortable around them and being who I was. With others, I could see how unhappy they were, having to look after children like me. They were just doing their job and nothing more, but I wanted something more. I needed to be loved and to feel that I was needed, and that was what I was missing.

Some of the children would talk about teachers they would like to be their mom and get attached to them. When the time came, the teachers moved on with their lives, and for us, all that was left was an emotional pain that sometimes never disappeared. For me personally, it was very difficult to understand some of the other children. Many of them had lost faith that one day their real family would come looking for them. For me, I never stopped believing, and not only that, I was sure and needed to believe that one day I would be the one looking for them and hopefully find them.

As the years went by, I turned seven and was transferred to an orphanage in the village of Preslavo, which is located on the Yugoslavian border north from the capital Pliska, two hours by car. The village was small and everybody knew everybody, so when a group of children like us arrived, we were their main subject for months.

Preslavo, 1981

The boarding school was mainly built for children travelling from local villages who couldn't afford to travel every day back home or their parents couldn't afford to have them during the week at home. Some of those children were at the boarding school on our arrival, and I didn't like the way we were being studied. They weren't sure what kind of children we were, and I knew that it was going to be a long way to go before we got on with them. None of them wanted to be associated with us or the "bastards' children," which was what some called us, and when the time came for us to be placed in our bedrooms, nobody wanted to be in the same room with us. However, there weren't enough beds and some had to be paired, like it or not, and I was one of them. I wasn't to question why I had to share a bed with someone who wet herself at night, which I found out eventually meant a smack in the face and being told to "grow up." I wasn't allowed to ask questions of any sort. So I had to accept the fact that in my first year at the orphanage school, I had to share my bed with a person who looked down on me for my skin color.

Almost every morning I had to be showered with somebody present to watch me, which wasn't pleasant at all. I hated those times and the person responsible for showering me almost every morning before breakfast. When I was having my shower, the others were queuing for their breakfast, and then when they were covering the first lesson, I was eating my cold food. After walking into the classroom, all the children would be staring and laughing at me. I didn't like the situation I was in and decided to do something about it immediately because it was definitely affecting me being without friends, affecting my school performance and nutrition because my food and tea was always cold by the time I had it and often went without.

Sometimes I would get into a fight with the hope that we would be put into separate beds, yet that never happened and my frustration turned to anger. Then one night, after everyone was asleep, I awoke the person in my bed to visit the toilet with me, resulting in all the children awakening in the middle of the night, one going hysterical for being woken up, another thinking it was morning already and started dressing up for school while talking loud enough for the night teacher to hear and run straight away to the room. I didn't make it to the toilet because my teacher was already standing in the doorway looking at me with scary eyes. I knew what was coming and there was no place to run, so I just stood up and took all the savage punches in the stomach and my face. Then he asked me to take my shirt off and started using a cable which he continued punishing me with savagely. Most of the children had taken cover under the blankets, pretending to be asleep while I was screaming in tears. I can't remember how I went to bed and how I got up the following day, but at school the next day, one of the teachers had noticed all the bruises I had and reported it to the headmaster who quickly reacted and asked for the teacher to be suspended and I never saw him again after that.

Life in the orphanage was very *dysfunctional*, yet in some ways, it helped shape me to become the person I am today. After the abuse, many teachers became more aware of how vulnerable I was, mainly due to my skin color, and spent more time around me ensuring I was okay. Of course, some of the children became jealous and started to avoid me. Some said I had a big mouth and started calling me monkey. They stopped inviting me to participate in their games, and I was invited if there was a situation where an additional member was required and then I could be that extra if there was nobody else. I didn't like to be second choice to anyone and quickly started working on my abilities in football and basketball. I knew if I was to make it in the team I had to be the best, so I practiced hard with the ball, either in football or basketball. I had the speed and awareness that many lacked, and that made me favorite each time when teams were selected for either game. I also never refused anyone who needed my help. Sometimes at class someone had a problem resolving a theory and I was there to help, and before I knew it, I had established myself as the person whom people could count on.

The locals didn't stay far behind, and I would start doing their shopping and stocking their firebricks for winter. Often after that I would be given some sweets, and that would make my day and even more when I shared my sweets with others. I have to say it was equal joy the attention I have received from the locals in the village and they from me. Other days after school there was always plenty to do, like helping in the kitchen with cutting the potatoes and peeling onions, which was very unpleasant at times. Sometimes I would be sent to the village to buy some ingredients or just to the orphanage to request something, and this was how I would be generally helping. I would get good recommendations for my help from the locals without knowing and was not surprised when they would call me by name and ask me to help them with the shopping, which they couldn't do because of bad *arthritis* or nobody to look after the chickens for whatever reason, and I would never refuse.

Often after I'd helped them, they would try to arrange with me for the next day after school to help with the same or something else for that matter. Before I knew it, I was committed to do all sorts throughout the week and even more that I could handle. Some of those people would have adopted me if it was just down to my wish, but they were old, and the way the system worked it should be them looking after me, not the other way around. When I wasn't busy helping in the afternoons, I would be involved in a game of basketball or football at the school yard. Children from the village would force themselves to play and we would have no choice but to let them. None of us was strong enough or confident to challenge them, and if they wanted the ball, then they would have the ball. I would always play for the boarding school team that most of the time was on the losing side. Kind of good in a way, considering what would have happened if we had won. Some of the local kids would have one of us do things we didn't like, and there wasn't much any of us could do to stop it—things like me punching someone in the face, and I wouldn't do it and then they would punch back at me.

Most times I would be left out of it because some of them were related grandchildren or children to the women in the village that I was helping. Of course, they would scare me if I ever opened my mouth to someone or their families. We were scared of them and maybe some of the teachers too, so in a way, maybe I should have said something, but I never did. Those games would normally occur during the weekends, and the teachers would be busy with their own hobbies, such as if it was a woman teacher, she would be most likely doing her nails or a male teacher would be reading a newspaper. In either case, they wouldn't be pleased for us to interrupt their afternoon! Other weekends when everyone was in bed for their afternoon "kip," I would jump out through the bathroom window and run on the black road that led to the back side of the school. I would get in through the small hole in the grid, and once inside, I would play basketball on my own for a few hours. I have to say that it was very naughty and if I had gotten caught would have led to my dismissal and being sent away to another boarding school with a bad reputation, which I wouldn't have wanted to happen. I would have one eye on the view as well because from where I was playing, I could see the road that led down to the orphanage, so if there was any movement, I would quickly run to the orphanage and nobody would have noticed that I was out.

Often, what would happen was that after the two hours of kip in the afternoon on weekends, the teacher would unlock the main door to the orphanage and then go and knock on the bedroom doors. Most children would carry on sleeping and others would be already out and screaming with the first knock on the door, and this was when I would go running the same way back unnoticed on the black road. If I did get to my room when the other children had just woken up, they wouldn't know what to think especially that I had jumped out through the bathroom window.

I also had a passion for music, and by the age of ten, I had my own gramophone with over twenty records. I bought it with my saved money, which I received every year from the government. I have to say I was very proud of myself and my choice of how I spent my money. Other children spent their money on sweets and some toys that didn't last long because they were exchanging among themselves; only mine lasted, and that created some disturbance because I had something that was mine and they didn't. Not that there weren't toys; those were kept in a locker, and the key was held by the teacher. But not many of the children understood how to play certain games, and fights would begin, caused by one accusing another of cheating and in the process a part would break or go missing. However, I did provide lots of good moments using my gramophone for occasions, such as someone's birthday party or around Christmas, where all of us without families to go to could only appreciate each other' s company.

Some of the teachers had never thanked me for making it easy for them to count us all before exchanging shifts as we would be all in the living room before going to bed and I played my records at that time. Keeping that gramophone wasn't easy as most children wanted to get their hands on it and I was determined to stop them. There wasn't a safe area for me to hide my gramophone so it had to be on my bedside table, and literally anyone at any time could come and play with it. I thought I was smart by hiding the records under my mattress and hoped that nobody would find them there only for someone to do so. One day after school, I went back to my room and found one of my records that was special to me being moved from the bed near the window where the sun had damaged it. My record of Madonna was damaged, and I have to say my frustration was unspeakable and right at that moment I just wanted to fight the person who did it. I had to arrange with the teachers to keep it in their rooms during the day when I was at school and in the evenings I could have it back only with the condition that I wasn't going to play music after eight.

The gramophone wasn't the only thing that kept me busy after school. I can't remember how that even started, but from somewhere, I have found an empty album and I turned it into a catalogue. There I had attached photographs of sports personalities from all different areas of sports, from football to tennis, and I was so proud of it. Mainly my supply would come from rubbish, some old magazines torn apart, and it helped a lot being in the area I lived. The village was located at the border of Yugoslavia, and over ten lorries per day would come to Preslavo driving from West Europe and leave rubbish behind for locals to clean. Sometimes the locals would ask me to help, and I would be there to help and find whatever my eyes have never seen before. I don't know what was the real reason for me collecting all these old magazines; sometimes I thought it was the love for sports and getting to know players by names and countries, sometimes even pictures of movie stars, other times it would be nostalgia for a different better life.

I had finished my album collection in a short period of time and was proudly starting to show it to the others, and since the album wasn't as heavy as my gramophone, therefore it wasn't difficult to hide it or carry it in my bag to school and back every day and show it to children and teachers. Whenever I felt depressed, I would look into it and start dreaming about knowing those people and wishing to see them on TV perhaps one day. Not that we had much what to see on newspaper or TV in the orphanage and not that we were allowed to watch anything at any time without permission. Sometimes we would be forced to watch the telly, like when the funeral of former Russian president Leonid Brejnev was shown, we had to be there to watch it from start to finish. I didn't complain then even though I was only eight years old at the time and didn't have a clue to what was going on. Another night I had to stay with a few other children watching the *Murder in Baker Street*, some bloody English horror, not that this was my choice, and after that it gave me sleepless nights. Also that night during the movie, the electricity was cut off and surely I shouldn't be watching this because I was only a child. For weeks, I have tried to clear out of my mind the horrifying images that I had seen and thanked God they never affected me—well, at least not that I know of. Other times when the choice would be mine, when the teachers weren't around, I would pick something like a sport or some Russian drama about how people died patriotically for their country during the war times and I would always end up crying a tear and the others would laugh at me. I have to say watching these movies did improve my Russian language skills, not that I didn't have to spend one afternoon by myself with the Russian teacher for over an hour trying to teach me a Russian poem that I was going to be examined on the following day by the same person while the others were playing a game of ball without me, regardless of the fact that I was the crucial player of the team.

That same teacher had found me hidden under my bed a few years back because I was being abused by some children calling me bad names, and she made me feel good about myself. So this is why I made a little effort to learn the language she so loved, and I have to say that after a while, I did find use of it. One summer, we were on holiday to the Black Sea in a small village of Ravda, where we shared camp with children from the city of Kostroma in USSR. It was so nice to know I could use the language in a game where we didn't really need to talk as it was all about passing the ball and scoring. Other times we didn't have to talk at all as we were engaged in a game of basketball. I have to say they were almost as equally passionate about the game as I was. In one of these summer holidays to Ravda I had met my future coach in football, and I know that if it wasn't for his wife working on my teeth one day, I wouldn't have met him. He happened to be coaching women in football, among them young girls my age. I definitely hoped to make an impression before the holiday was over. I have to say that wasn't difficult for me for I had the confidence I needed at the time and the basic skills that obviously had been noticed by the coach. I was on a show every day with the ball until he came to me and offered me assistance on how to change something in my game if I wanted to be a better player one day. I expressed my desire to play for his team one day in the future when I leave the orphanage and move to live in Pliska, and he was very keen to have me too so we exchanged details and promised to stay in touch. This promise to play football for Levski Pliska ladies' football team gave me such a motivation to live upon for the next two or three years before I turned fifteen. In the meantime, some families had been interested in adopting me and sent a request regarding me. Whenever any interest comes along for any of the children, the director himself would ask the child to visit his office and then he would go with the speech on how it is in our interest to be adopted. It happened to me more times than I can remember, and I have to say I was a bit bored.

The teachers all knew I wasn't interested in being adopted, and some had sympathy for me. My answer was always no regardless of the temptations that were offered to me. Most of the other children would fight me to be in my position, and there I was throwing away opportunities of a better life. Some of the families that requested to know about me barely had the opportunity to talk to me directly, and others, like the one I specifically remember when I must have been only seven years old, a woman who took me by my hand and dragged me to an area near the river. I was bemused and scared by her behavior and the fact that she had to be alone with me in a place that I always hated going as a child didn't do any good for her intentions. Often when one wanted to meet with the child of their choice they would have a teacher present, but not on this occasion with me. There she stood and asked me if I wanted her to be my mother. I was very cool and remember saying that I wasn't interested and I am only waiting for my own mother. She then tried to reinforce her desire by offering me chocolate, which I took quickly, and she promised to give me even more if I would allow her to adopt me. I refused the chocolate or whatever was left of it, and she was really getting frustrated with me and grabbed me by the arm and led me back to the orphanage.

Another time, it was late at night and we were all asleep when the night teacher came into my room and woke me up. He commanded me to get dressed and be quiet because he did not want any of the other children to know what was happening. I wasn't sure what this was about and got dressed quickly, and the next thing knew, I found myself sitting in the back of a car. We were on the road for almost three to four hours, and I remember being so tired and falling asleep almost immediately. When we eventually got to the apartment, I was half awake and realized that I didn't know the people that had taken me and what was happening to me. For the first time, I was a bit scared, if not traumatized. The man and the woman were charging around the small apartment looking for something while I was standing in the corridor unsure of what I was supposed to do. Not long after that, I was put into a big bed in which I was feeling so comfortable and was just about to close my eyes when the man slid under my blanket to my shock. I was in fear; all this was very awkward for me. People that I had never met in my life before were about to share a bed with me. I assumed that all that was just a dream or I wanted to be, but it wasn't. The woman joined us in bed, and not before she switched off the main lights did I see her being all naked. Then she got herself comfortable next to me on my left side, and there it was me lying in bed between two adults.

The next day and the days after that for me were like hell in this apartment. I was being locked up during the big part of the day in the apartment all by myself, playing with some toys that probably belonged to some other kid before me. I would sit in the corridor for hours and hours, not knowing when one would come. I didn't eat breakfast and would eat only when they were back from work late in the afternoon. Very rarely would I be taken out of the apartment that had no TV or radio. I was missing my friends from the orphanage, and I was crying every day, begging them to take me back to the orphanage. They wanted me to call them Mom and Dad, and I couldn't or I didn't want to. They started calling me by a different name, something like "Emilia," and I wouldn't respond most of the time. The woman would be yelling at me a lot, and the man would argue with her and then the other way around. Until one day they decided to take me on a small holiday to Varna, one of the largest seaside resorts by the Black Sea.

On the way there, they argued a lot, pulling the car on the side of the road very often. I would pretend that I was driving the car and distracted myself away from their arguments. I would push the Klaxon by mistake, and they'd go mad with me and drive off. When we arrived at the camp in Varna, it was the last time I saw the woman. I was all by myself with the man, and that was when things started going wrong. At night, even though there were two beds, he would force himself to sleep in mine. I was fighting him, but he was too strong almost every night. I stopped eating, became weak, and he would force me to play with him. When we were in public areas, I would refuse to obey him, and after that when we were alone, he would beat me. Again, I would be left locked in the room and he would be out for the long part of the day. When he got back, he would be drunk and would often go to sleep or he would try to force me to do things I didn't like, and that was how one night the people that were staying next door to us heard me crying and came knocking on the door. The man had no other choice but to open the door and then I was hoping that somehow I could find a way to get away from him and go with the people next door, but that didn't happen as he managed to convince them there was nothing wrong and that I was crying because my mother had left me or something like that.

One day soon after that, he took me to the beach and made me go on an air mattress, and since many other children were playing in the water with them, I thought nothing of it. He also had one of his size and then we both got in the water. I have been many times in the river Tevna in Preslavo so I wasn't that scared of the water. However, I didn't know first thing about the sea and its depth, and I let myself relax on the air mattress under the full control of the man who had to hold my air mattress that had a rope attached to his so that I didn't get blown away by the sea waves. Next thing I remember was being in the water and screaming for help with no signs of the air mattress and nothing to hold myself on to—only me and the water. No sign of the man and nobody near me to help, and then it all went dark.

I woke up in a hospital, not remembering anything at all, and I looked around the room to find any clue as to where I was. I didn't recognize any of the faces as they were all women in my room, women that I have never seen before, and the one near my bed smiled at me when our eyes met. I smiled back at her as there was so much warmth in her eyes. She spoke to me and asked me how I felt, and before I even got to say something, a nurse ran into the room toward me with concern and put one hand on my forehead as if to check if I had a fever. Then she sat next to me on the bed and stared at me for a while before she asked me if I had any memory of what happened to me. I said that I couldn't remember and that everything was so cloudy in my head, and then she told me that I was admitted to the hospital two weeks back and that this was the first time I had come around.

She mentioned that I had been found collapsed on the floor in my bedroom at the orphanage and screaming, not making sense. For days I would stay in the room and only use the toilet when needed. The nurse would visit me every day, and her presence was always warm toward me.

There was more certain chemistry between us and only for me to spoil it. She asked me one day as I was coming back from the toilet in the corridor on the way to my room, holding my hand while we both sat on the bench, if I wanted her to adopt me. Saying yes to her would have been the right decision, but it didn't look that way to me back then. With all I had experienced, I had no trust in people. I had never felt so insecure in my life, and yet this woman was ready to adopt me, to offer me a home, something that I had always wanted. But she had two children, and for me being different, there was no way I would let myself being hurt again. I was different, and I have accepted that. I believed back then that my own kind wouldn't hurt me and I would be loved by them unconditionally.

In a few days' time, I would be back at the orphanage reunited with the rest of the children as though I had never been away. I resumed my study, having really dropped behind the rest, and the time wasn't enough for me; I had to stay after school and do catch-up while the others were playing. I would start fantasizing of the moment when I was going to leave the orphanage as an adult, then I would do whatever I wanted. But some questions had started to arise in my head, such as, what will happen when I leave the orphanage? I needed to ask someone, but I didn't know who to trust among the teachers. It was never going to be easy to ask any teacher about what would happen to me or the rest of us once we left the orphanage. There was one teacher I have always felt close to and comfortable talking about any subject that concerned me. I understood from her that it all depended on the grades we got in our final year. There was also the matter if you were boy or a girl because all the boys would be sent to a boarding school after secondary, specializing in becoming mechanics, and all the girls would be sent to a women's boarding school where they would learn to be tailors or whatever other jobs women do.

I have to say none of this appealed to me and I had to start thinking about my future. I didn't know how and from where to start, but I knew that I would start by finding my mother first. I knew nothing about her, as nobody had spoken about her and she was going to be hard to find. Besides that, I didn't even know where to look. However, fortune did come my way one afternoon. I was again one of the few left behind in the classroom, not having finished my homework for the next day, when my teacher decided she needed some fresh air and left behind on the desk some papers that she was working on. Not that I was curious what she was working on, but something just pushed me from the inside to go and have a look.

There was another boy with me in the room, and I told him not to say a word about this to anyone. As I got near the desk, first thing I saw was the name of one of the children I knew. With the speed of a lion, I went through all of them until I found what I wanted—my name. There it was, my mother's name. And my father's name, empty. I quickly wrote her name on the side of my hand, and to my disappointment, there wasn't an address. I was happy with the little I got, and while I was doing all this, the boy was looking through the window to check if anyone was coming. Just when I thought I had finished, he asked me to look for his mother's name. Luckily for him, she had an address, and I wrote it all down on a piece of paper for him.

I was happy and he was happy while I was putting everything back into its place. The teacher came back to the room, and I swear if we looked half bored before she left the room afterward, we were definitely the two happy to be left behind. I knew I had two years away from being sent to another boarding school and only God knows where that would be if my grades weren't good. If I was to share my plans with anyone, that would have been only one person, Emma. She has been my friend since kindergarten and also her parents living in Pliska was going to ease my situation for going there. Since I have been there before at their house, it would never occur on anyone's mind why I wanted to go there again. I was going to start my search for my mother from the hospital where I was born, and only me and Emma would know about it.

I knew she left me there and had signed all the papers while she was probably still in her pajamas. I didn't want to think of the reason why she'd left me for adoption, and I had to focus on what she would say when she saw me grown, perhaps with her regretting leaving me in a government institution and taking me back with her.

The right time eventually came for us to leave for Pliska; I was only visiting for the weekend and was supposed to be back on Sunday evening for the count. That was when children were being counted in the presence of the two teachers who were doing something like a handover. In Pliska, we had to ask people how to get to the hospital where I was born. At the end, we got to a hospital and asked at the reception if there was a woman called Sonya Ivanova. After a long silence and a puzzled look at me, the woman said, "There is a woman Mariana Ivanova. Should I call her?"

I had to think for a while and then said, "Yes." As she had the same surname, therefore she could be related or something. I was excited and hoping that the woman would know my mother or at least help me find her.

We were sitting in the waiting room for a long time before a woman approached us, wishing to speak with me. She had a rather concerned face and pulled me to one side where only I could hear.

"I am sorry you had to come all the way here, but I am not your mother." I was looking into her eyes, trying or hoping to find something in her eyes that was familiar to me. But there was nothing, and her voice was cold like an iceberg so I have stopped listening to what she was saying and walked away.

I walked down the street silently with disappointment as Emma followed behind, not daring to say a word that I might find upsetting. We got back to her house sometime in the afternoon, only to find that the house door was locked and no way for us to get in. Often, Emma's parents would leave her wandering around the house while they were zooming the street bins for anything that could be recycled and sometimes they would even take Emma with them. In this case, we went to a place called Student Town as it wasn't very far from their house. It had a big stadium where we found lots of children on this Saturday afternoon playing football, and it wasn't a problem for Emma and me to join. I was the goalkeeper and was taking my position seriously when a man approached me from behind and distracted me with a hello.

This is when I saw for the first time someone who looked like me but with much darker skin. He smiled at me from a distance. I stepped one foot back looking at him, not knowing what to say when all the other children ran toward me, screaming, "Monkey, monkey!" at him. Then a part of me woke up, not from the shock that I was seeing a black man for the first time in my life, but from the words said toward the man who looked a little bit like me and had an effect on me too. I knew this man was a stranger to me and yet I felt a bond between us. The thought of that scared me too. I wasn't ready to meet that other part of me yet, only when I've started looking for my mother. I was scared because I had started to realize then that the other part of me was black and this was why other children had called me "monkey" all the time. The man obviously paid no attention to what the children were calling him as his total focus was on me. The children eventually gave up as they saw he was way too busy with me and ran off playing football, but not me.

He took my hand and asked me, "What is your name?" I answered straight away. Then he wanted to know where my father was from, and all I did was shake my head, not knowing the answer. We were approached by a woman with blond hair who seemed rather friendly with him and then it was my turn to run off. They waited on the side hoping for me to go back and talk to them, but I didn't.

That experience with the black man changed the way I was seeing myself at the time and certainly showed me that I was not the only one with that skin color, but in the village where I lived, unfortunately I was the only one. I never talked with anybody about this and not even Emma because no matter what, she and I were still very different. I was mixed race, that was certain, and talking about the black side of me with any white person felt uncomfortable. I was told that black people originated from Africa, and yet at school we never learned anything about the history of the black continent like it almost didn't exist. So in a way, that part of me didn't exist either, but it was hidden somewhere and with time would come out.

I was encouraged to continue to do well at school as the years were rolling, and I had only one year left before graduation. I was fourteen. Lots had happened then, like my friend Emma had left the orphanage and moved to live with her parents in the capital, where she never continued with her school; that would've been the last I saw of her. A boy from my class died swimming in the river Tevna in front of me and others one afternoon; it took almost a week of searching to find his body and then we all had to attend his funeral. That was a very traumatic experience for anyone at a young age, and for me, that was the time when I realized how short life could be.

I have seen in the houses of some elderly people over the years old photographs of people that have left the world, but I never dared to ask why or how they died. In my own way, I was scared to know more about what happens when someone dies, but deeply I wished they were loved and had happy lives and somebody to remember them. Most of the people in the village who died were taken to the nearby church that was right next to the school, and sometimes the body would be left inside the church for relatives and friends to say their last goodbyes with the door to the church left open. Once during a game of football, the ball went over into the churchyard, and though we were not allowed to go there without permission, being brave, I quickly jumped over to find the door to the church open.

Until that moment in my life, I was never inside a church, and my first feelings were very confusing and I was fearful of the unknown behind the door. The warmth I felt inside the church felt so safe, and I was hypnotized by all the graphics on the wall. I couldn't take my eyes off the cross with Jesus Christ and felt like I was being watched, but there was nobody around so I ran out with the ball scared, back toward the school with mixed feelings. That feeling of being watched would follow me for a long time, and I would never share this feeling with other children, just in case they thought I had lost my mind. However, I was intrigued by the spiritual life, and no books were around in the orphanage about any religions whatsoever and alongside that I had started to experience a different kind of feeling toward boys too. I knew nothing about relationships between boys and girls and was ever so embarrassed to think about it, let alone try to speak with any teacher about it.

One of my very first memories associated with a boy and a girl comes at a very early stage of my life, and I don't think it was right what I had witnessed at the time. It was one summer, and we were sent away from the orphanage for a month in a summer camp somewhere in the mountains. Boys and girls sometimes would be put to sleep in the same rooms, and nothing was thought of it. But for me, it was a weird thing, and I often refused to take my clothes off in front of boys and would go to bed without undressing. There were boys older than me and most of the other girls, and whenever the teachers would go to bed, they would come to our bedrooms and start forcing some of the girls to strip. I was always against it and hardly kept my mouth shut when it came to any forceful violence. I hated the boys from the other orphanages because they were well known for bad reputation and even some of the teachers couldn't cope with them. They often used the boys from my orphanage to do things they would never think of doing or had the courage to do so if they wish to. In this case, they forced one of the boys from my orphanage to sleep with one of the girls from the other orphanage. Both refused to do it and got kicked and bitten until they obeyed at the end.

For me, that image will haunt me for a long time and certainly didn't help with boys much. But there was this boy that I liked and I wasn't sure if the feeling was mutual, so I sent him a note one day through another boy who was a few years younger and had no clue what it was about. So he got my note where to meet and came to the appointed place. It was late afternoon, and we were allowed to play in the orphanage yard until the teachers' handover. He didn't talk much as I have already noticed that about him, and this was what attracted me about him, but somebody had to make the move first. So I started the conversation about how much I liked him and wanted to know if he shared the same feelings. No, he didn't! He came to tell me in the face that he liked someone else and likes to only be friends with me. I was upset, yes, I was hurting and embarrassed with myself and next time, I knew, should do better. I left it that way, avoided personal feelings, and focused completely on my final grades that would decide which school I had a chance to apply to.

I had only one thing on my mind, and that was to enter myself into any sports academy. I knew that wasn't an option and I was hoping for something to happen, and something did lead to it. There was a marathon organized a few weeks later, and I was put down to run in it. I didn't see it back then as an opportunity, but I gave my whole heart and won it out of fifty-something children from different schools in the region that was held in the city of Drayan back in 1987.

Everyone at school and the orphanage was so proud of me, and I received very positive applause from my sport teacher who put a word to the headmaster about my abilities in sports and that I should be given the opportunity to apply in the sports academy of Lion Pliska in Pliska. Everyone was behind the idea, and I was on the seventh moon. One of the teachers had registered my name as a candidate for the new season in the sports academy with basketball, and I was to have a preliminary test in 100 meters running and showing skills with the ball on the pitch. I knew there was nothing in my way to achieving those results and winning a place in the girls' basketball team for the next year 1988, and I gave hours and days of running and timed at the same time. I would practice on the basketball pitch every day on my own from shooting range to dribbling and running with the ball between my legs, bouncing and scoring from outside the D area. I was confident that I was going to make it, and nobody could convince me otherwise.

The day came for my interview with the girls' basketball team coach for Lion Pliska. One of the teachers drove me in her car to Pliska, and it was there next to me at the time of my observation. I passed my tests, and with a smile on both teachers' faces, I knew I'd done well. Now the rest was for them to sort, and this is where it all went wrong. The sports academy offered a place to live from Monday to Friday only, and it became a big issue the fact that I wouldn't be able to stay on my own in the academy. The teacher that was with me was also disappointed, and when we got back to Preslavo, the headmaster was absorbed in phone calls trying to find a solution on where I could stay over the weekends if I was to choose to stay with the sports academy. However, there was no other way but for me to give up that dream and take on whatever came next.

Graduation time came so soon, and the excitement of a new life ahead of me and the others was something that some were ready for and others not. I was most certainly ready, and at the same time I was going to miss everyone in the orphanage who had spent years of looking after me, years of putting up with me, years of joy, and years of disappointments. They also knew that the time would come when we would grow up and have to move out to a different place with a different life. Most of the staff was very sad to see us leaving, not knowing if they would see us ever again. Promises of "stay in touch" and "come back" were said, but not every child would keep that promise. To me personally, I knew I wasn't going to come back for many years. I needed to move on, and thinking of the people I would leave behind would make it only worse and as far I was concerned, a new chapter of my life was about to start. I knew that the school I was going to start in September was in Pliska and was called Stoyan Petrov, specializing in textile and design, and that the orphanage where I was going to stay was an hour away on a bus.

Orphanage Hristo Botev in Pavlovo, 1988

We were dropped literally in front of the building in Pavlovo at nighttime, a place well known for its mineral water. From the looks of the dark building, it was obvious that we were not expected to arrive that day. All the rooms were dark, and movement in or around couldn't be heard. The teacher I was with had to make a few phone calls from the phone booth that was located on the other side of the road. After that, we had to wait for a man to appear and let us in. He was showing us around the bedrooms and where the bathroom was using only a torch.

Before I could even ask, the teacher beat me to it and asked the man with the torch if there was a way to switch on the mains. The answer was negative and followed by an explanation that there was no need since it was going to be only me in the building until September when school starts and all the children would arrive from the provinces. So I had to stay for a month and a half with no power, completely on my own in a three-story building with more than thirty rooms and basements. I had been given a key to the front door of the orphanage and told strictly not to let anyone in at any time. I knew that wouldn't be a problem, but what would have been was my going out. I had nobody that I knew there, and whenever I showed myself briefly, everyone would be staring at me as though I didn't belong there. It was hard because I needed to buy food, and I mean sandwiches mainly and chocolates to keep me going for days. I had no desire to be out there on the street where drunk men would be shouting.

Sometimes I could hear them from my bedroom window and they wouldn't suspect that someone was in the orphanage. My room was on the third floor, and at night I would use a candle so that I could read. I had no other distraction, and I was missing my music that I had left back in the orphanage in Preslavo. I missed the other children a lot and kept wondering if they were missing me too. Then in moments like this I start realizing that Preslavo was where I had spent eight years of my life and more or less the people there were like my family and then I'd start thinking of my mother and being so close to her as I was now living in Pliska. As the days went by and my daily routine was the same, the excitement was growing inside me that very soon the place would be lively and filled with children and I would have someone to talk to.

The first person that came to the orphanage was very early in the morning, and I was woken up by the sound of slamming door. I intended to find who was in the building apart from me, and I put one ear next to the door, trying to listen. I didn't want to expose myself yet and hoped that whoever it was would call out for me first because surely they would know that somebody was staying there while everyone was on summer holiday. I stood there for like ten minutes, and nothing that I could hear could overcome my fears of whatever danger there might be.

Walking to the bottom of the staircase, I then heard a noise coming from the basement, a place where breakfast, lunch, and dinner was served. Somebody was there doing something, and I had to investigate. I found a man loading cases of milk and other supplies; of course, he was the deliveryman, and he was surprised to see me there too. We had a little talk, or I had a little talk with him of "who are you" or "how are you," as he was trying to get on with his duties and then left. For me, it was great that someone was around; plus, I could get to know where the food was kept, and the good thing with that was that I would finally have electricity.

He left and locked the door behind and I was all on my own again, but this time, I could use hot water to shower and do my laundry and get to read my book in a normal light. A few days only to go before teachers and children would arrive and me reading my book, when there was a little knock on the window. Fuck! I didn't realize that I had left the lights on, and my head start speeding! I turned off the lights and waited for the next sound; surely I didn't imagine the knock on the window. I stood there frightened to death of who might be there and why on earth I was so stupid to reveal myself. Of course, it's got to be some of these drunk men that were coming for the past few weeks or it could be the guy that came earlier and who even had a key to the place, but he wouldn't have the key to my room. However, he can still break the door and get in and I wouldn't be able to do anything to stop him. Jesus! I knew that if I hear any sound inside the building I would open the window and scream as loud as I could, and I am damn sure somebody would hear me. Another little tapping on the window followed, like someone was at the window, and there was.

Somebody was almost whispering for me to open the window, and I stayed as quiet as possible until whoever it was gave up and left. I stayed awake for most of the night, wondering if that person would come back and do the same the following evening and what I should do next time he comes back. I didn't see his face and wouldn't be able to recognize him if I saw him. Maybe he knew my face from the times when I went to the shop and back, or maybe he didn't. I was convinced that I should stay indoors the following day and not give a chance to whoever to have a look at me. I stayed indoors as promised to myself and did everything but think of the person from last night. The chances were that he might be back again or not and I wouldn't take any chances, and I decided to sleep in a different room this time. Different floor and room that faces the street for easy exit if needed.

I had no problems and went to sleep, knowing that the next day would bring things back to normal. The day followed and, as I would have expected, started with banging on the doors and children talking in the corridors. I showed myself, and their faces showed surprise at finding me in the building. I didn't waste time and started introducing myself as they did also. All were interested where I was from, and some started touching my hair with admiration while I was busy answering all the questions. All of them were girls more or less my age, and for all of them, this was going to be their first year in the orphanage and they all had families.

The time came when we all were gathered in the lunchroom and asked which school we were attending, and those from the same school had to step to one side. I was the only one that was attending Stoyan Petrov and was left on the side to wait for much longer while all the other girls had to be allocated to their rooms. The girls that I had met in the corridor before had been selected together, and to my regret, I wasn't going to be in the same room with them. At the end when there was only me left, I was told that there were two more girls to come in the next few days and they would have to share a room with me. The same happened on the boys' floor, and there were rules that boys should not go to girls' rooms and vice versa. I was on my own for the next few days, thinking how nice it would be to have roommates and friends to share things with, but I was completely wrong about that.

Both girls were sixteen, and this was their second year at this orphanage. Both came from troubled families and went to the same school. Sharing the room with them wasn't exactly what I would have imagined, and yet I didn't mind much as long as there was somebody in the room. They hardly spoke to me, and one of them forced me to change beds because mine belonged to her from the year before. At night when everyone would go to sleep, the two of them would jump on the bed that was next to the window and have it wide open so that they could smoke. I didn't know if I should say something about that to anyone, but I certainly didn't want to give people the impression that I was someone that can't be trusted. The drunk people that I so got used to seemed to be friends with these girls, as almost every night one of them would climb somehow two levels on the outside and reach the window so close that you could smell the alcohol. Of course, what they were doing did have a negative effect on me at school as I would miss out on the material at class while deep asleep. The teacher would have me in the headmaster's office, trying to find out why I was falling asleep each time at class, but they would never get to the bottom of it and left me to it. The headmaster probably knew about my situation being left for adoption and was sympathetic in most cases. To the children in my class, I was weird, and most did not want anything to do with me after school. My daily routine would be getting up for school at 6:00 a.m. followed by a quick breakfast at the orphanage and then catching my bus from the main square in Pavlovo, where most buses would start their routes. Some of the children from the orphanage would be waiting at the bus stop, and whenever I would try to make eye contact or smile at them, they would turn their heads in the opposite direction, pretending they hadn't seen me. I would get on my bus and be the only person from the orphanage to be on it for a long time in silence until the bus reached the final destination. I would transfer to a tram for about ten minutes, which would stop right in front of the school. Sometimes in the mornings I would not be able to get on the tram because it was full and I would walk or run and take my chance at being late. When I got to school, I would have a few minutes left and would go inside the canteen where most of my classmates would be there, but as soon as I was spotted, they would find something to laugh about me.

I was completely on my own, and I was missing my friends from the orphanage in Preslavo and had no way to go back there without permission from the headmaster. I was under eighteen, only two years before becoming an adult, and by doing anything stupid, I could get sent to one of the worst institutions for children in the country. So whenever I got provoked by others, I just tried to ignore it and walked away; and to make life easy, I stopped going to the canteen. Not that I was going there to buy because I never had money. I was never given any money at that time for anything. I didn't even know if I was entitled to receive any from the government since I was an orphan. At least that was what happened when I was in Preslavo; I would receive ten Bulgarian leva every month, which I would choose to save.

Anyway, I stopped going to the canteen and spent the time in the classroom before everyone else arrived. I would make sure I had all my papers with me and rehearsed my homework. I had nothing else in my life but orphanage and school, and that was that. Sometimes in the evenings I would watch whatever was on the telly, something that was watched by everyone in the room. The room was also used for games when nobody was watching, and some would be playing table tennis and others would be playing cards with a small bet on the side. That is how I got to know that many of the boys in the orphanage were involved in sports after school, like wrestling. Some of them were semiprofessional, and they had to spend almost the same amount of time in the club as in the school. I thought about it that since they can do that after school, definitely I would like to do football too. I didn't waste time one day after school. I got on the bus toward the national stadium, following the directions I was given by somebody at school. I got there and without too much fuss got myself in the team; they didn't require any signature or identification card, and all I showed was my skills. I was proud with myself that I had gone that far on my own, meeting with the coach and doing my best to return to the orphanage without getting lost, almost making it to dinner. The teachers didn't take any notice of my absence at the canteen or else I would have heard something. The good thing about this orphanage was that you could be miles away while the teachers were doing their handover and nobody told you anything. The only problem was once the door to the orphanage was closed at eight sharp, that was that—no opening after that.

I had that happening to me once after a training. I missed my connection with the second bus, and that led to missing the main bus to the orphanage. When I got there, the door was locked and I had no place to go. I was forced to knock on the door and shout very loudly below some of the bedroom windows, and from the lights in the rooms, I could see that most children were still up. One eventually showed his head out through the window, and I begged him to tell the teacher that I was outside. The teacher showed no interest whatsoever in the fact that I was a girl waiting outside in the dark and had no place to go to. I just sat outside on the staircase believing that I would be kept in the cold for a lesson for some time and then would be let in and told off, but none of this happened. I waited until all the lights went off, and I was on my own in the dark. I could hear voices approaching from the train station that was only a few minutes north of people who were going home and those for whom the night had just began. I sat there quietly in the dark, still hoping for the door to open, when somebody approached me and all I could see was the light of the cigarette in his hand. He noted that I was sitting by myself and asked me why I didn't go inside. I explained, and he looked at his watch, pointing to me the time, something past ten o'clock. I was starting to get worried for myself and being on my own with a complete stranger who to that point didn't do anything and I had nothing against him being there. I wouldn't like to be completely on my own, not really, so we engaged in conversation and at the end he offered me a place to stay the night. I was so tired that I said yes; after all, the place was only ten minutes away. He happened to be a local boy who lived with his parents in their house and wouldn't mind if I spent the night there. What he said happened to be true, as his parents were next door snoring away like I had never heard before!

The following morning, he did keep his promise and took me to school directly and introduced himself again as Ivan. I could tell he was much older than the guys in the orphanage, and what I liked about him was he wasn't embarrassed when he was with me and made me feel comfortable with myself. I started to trust him and see him whenever I could. He would come all the way to the stadium where I played football and watch me, and yet we were not yet together. We had a few kisses, and that was it even though I knew he would like to have something more. I was inexperienced and had nobody to ask for advice on how to deal with a boy in a relationship. The teachers weren't bothered if I was there or not; nobody was there to check my grades at school. Things that I needed like tampons and every now and then money to buy underwear or clothes for the winter that I had were those that I took with me from Preslavo and the rest I had to borrow money with.

As time went by, December came and one day I was visited in my bedroom by one of the teachers. She had to inform me that the orphanage would be closed for about ten days for the holidays so I should find a place to stay. I explained that I have no place to stay and it was fine by me to be on my own in the orphanage, and she categorically said that it wouldn't possible and I should find a place to stay somewhere. I felt sad and almost wanted to cry as images from the years in Preslavo with all the other orphans together celebrating Christmas and New Year was all just a shadow of memories. I was in Pliska, a big city where I know only one person with whom I can stay and which wasn't guaranteed because he wasn't my family. My life wasn't what I thought it would be, and I had no control over it. I had to find a place to stay, and Ivan said yes. His parents were out of town, and he shared the apartment with his sister and her boyfriend. I was introduced to her on Christmas eve, and she accepted me with warmth.

Ivan was very open-minded and liked me for who I was, or at least that was what he said. He did, however, have a bad habit, and that was alcohol and cigarettes. Whenever I saw him, he always smoked or had drunk a few vodkas in the day. The time I spent at his house was great. We had lots of fun and went to the cinemas, out in his car driving anywhere we wanted. He even tried to teach me to drive, and I struggled big-time! Before we knew it, I had to go back to the orphanage like nothing happened. I would agree that with the way I was treated by the teachers, it was as though I wasn't their concern whatever happened to my life. The ignorance they have showed me just motivated me more and more to want to live somewhere else, perhaps move out with Ivan. I was almost sixteen and not eighteen, so I couldn't do what I wanted yet. At school, everything continued as normal and my grades were not perfect, but neither were they the worst in class. I know I could have done better if I had wished to pay more attention in class, but the teachers at school didn't care that half of the time I was hungry in their classes. I had no money to buy lunch for myself and watched most of the children eating and after each break return to the classroom with an empty stomach. None of them knew what I was going through, and I didn't want sympathy, but understanding only. I did my best, and that was all I could do.

One evening after a long day, I was relaxing in my bedroom all alone when the night teacher knocked on the door and waited outside to be let in by me. He said to me that a few days before, he had shared a taxi with an African man to whom he had spoken about me and that this man would like to meet with me if I wished to. I didn't know what to say to that and promised to think about it. Time passed by, and Easter was around the corner when I received an invitation through my teacher to visit the African man and his family for the holidays. I was confused and happy that someone wanted to spend time with me and get to know me. From the teacher, I learned that his name was Peter and he was from Nigeria, married to a Bulgarian woman with whom he had a son of seven years. I took the invitation and waited for Peter to arrive the following day. I had my bag packed and stood outside the orphanage waiting for him to arrive, and he wasn't long. My first impression of him was very good as he introduced himself. He explained to me why he thought I should visit his family. He told me that being mixed race could be very difficult to deal with in a country such as Bulgaria and that many people like him had been attacked in Student Town where he lived and some were even killed. I didn't know if I should take this information as a warning or just a story from a man whom I had only just met. Peter had his own car, which was good for moving from A to B without being too much on people's radar, especially after what he had told me. Only twenty-something minutes of drive and we were in front of his apartment in Student Town, where you could see heads looking out the windows as if they had all been told of my visit. It was amazing when I got out of the car to see his little look-alike boy running toward Peter and grabbing his leg. Peter was delighted and lifted the boy high above his shoulders as he was smiling. Seeing this made me feel good about being there with this black man and his son.

A woman was heading toward us, and she greeted me first by my name and reached her hand out of her pocket. "Hi," she said, smiling at me. "My name is Elena, and I am Peter's wife."

I greeted her back and realized who she was before she even said it. She wanted to know if I had a nice journey and said how happy she would be for me to stay with them. All I did was nod my head in agreement to what she was saying. My mind was totally on the whole new experience for me, to live with an interracial family, and all the emotions started flying high. I got in the apartment and felt the warmth and family comfort everywhere my eye could see. The table was set for four people and ready to be served, and I realized it was going to be lunchtime soon. It was a strange feeling to sit and have lunch with a proper family. Peter put my bag on the floor and pointed to my bedroom as he was walking toward it. I followed him to see the room and liked it very much. I noticed another bed there too. Peter obviously read my mind and said that this was where his son sleeps and so we would become good friends, something I would love. In my mind to that point, I never wished to have a brother or sister, yet seeing the young son of Peter and Elena so much like me made me wish I had one that looked just like him. John—that was the young boy's name—followed me around almost everywhere after lunch. Obviously to him I was some kind of entertainment with whom he wanted to play. I had no problem with this, except for the fact that I really wasn't very good in playing games with children younger than me. In the orphanage in Preslavo, I would play games like chess and domino and barely touch any of the toy cars and dolls; that simply wasn't me. Pretending that I am driving a little toy car and making some sounds and crushing it on the floor or take the clothes off a doll and brushing the hair or whatever else children did with toys wasn't me, simple as that.

However, with John, he had lots of different toys that I had only seen in some of the old rubbish magazines that I used to find in Preslavo after school. He had Legoland game and many others, but it was the first one that I wanted to explore. Before we knew it, we were involved in the game, passionately laughing at the creativity of each other. I didn't know as much as he did, but it was fun. His parents let us spend time alone as long as we both wanted, and every now and then Peter or Elena would show up to check if we wanted a snack, knowing that we wouldn't let off the game for a second.

Just like that, when you are having a great time with someone, the time goes so fast. Peter and Elena had organized a little party for me before I went back to the orphanage, and I was very touched and shed a tear or two without them noticing. At the party, there were other interracial families with girls also looking like me, some my age, others much younger. Seeing those families happy made me realize that I could have the same if I was brave enough to find my own parents. So I wished the same for myself when I blew the candles on my cake. The rest of the day I played with some girls, and not for a second would I be looked in a strange way. To me, it felt so natural to be around them without being awkward about myself, and just like that, the Easter holiday was over and I had to return to the orphanage in Pavlovo. Peter did, of course, promise to stay in touch with me and expressed how much he and his wife loved my company, and if I ever needed any support or anything else, they will be there. Knowing that someone was there for me was a great feeling because it was not something they would do out of duty to me. They also gave me encouragement to believe that one day I could also find my parents, and Peter strongly believed that my father wouldn't in a million years abandon me for anything in this world! He explained to me how different the African culture is to the European and how family was all that mattered to them more than money and success. I, however, didn't know anything about my parents so I couldn't make any judgment on this.

Back at the orphanage, things weren't the same for me, the better taste of experience with people who cared about me and the love they showed me almost tempted me to run far away somewhere like Africa maybe. I have never felt so lonely as at that point in my life, and all I could think of was my mother, questions spinning in my head with no one to answer them. At least I had the promise to visit Peter's family again, and that promise kept me going for the next few weeks. I was more comfortable with myself after meeting with the mixed-race girls, who were just like me, and the way they were interacting with other children showed me that they were proud of their skin color. I became more confident about myself and my origin, holding my head up and stopped acting like there was something wrong about me or at least trying to act normal. Sometimes I was successful, and other times I wasn't and maybe I did come across to other children as a bit more arrogant, which wasn't really the intention. For instance, one time after school, I decided to walk a few bus stops and have fresh air. I loved walking, but that was something I haven't done since Preslavo, where I would walk free in the village and everyone would know me and greet me with a smile. However, here in the big city, I felt uncomfortable glancing at anyone on the street.

As I was walking, a group of young boys and girls walked toward me, pushing each other in play, followed by laughs. I was about to pass them when a heavy punch hit me in the face, and I fell to the ground. I got up on my knees and looked at them while they were laughing at me and calling me "monkey" to which words I didn't react. What they said after that was something that hurt me even more than anything, that I didn't belong in "their country" and that I should go back to Africa where I belonged. I agreed with that part, sadly even though I was always told that I was Bulgarian and yet I was different. I didn't belong there and I did want to go back to Africa, and how much they were right about that. The trouble was, I didn't know how to do it. I didn't know anything about my father, and frustration was mixed with anger that I was so weak and embarrassed with myself of the fact that I was so different and every day there was somebody to remind me of that. I certainly didn't feel safe on the streets anymore, and in the next months, I moved only with transport from school to the training grounds and from there straight on the bus to the orphanage.

At the team where I trained football, all the girls were nice to me and I put that down to the fact that I was supposed to be related to some of the great players of all time like Pelé and Zico. Most of the girls in the team admired my dedication to the game and the hard work I always put into my practice. I never had any bad word with any of them, and whenever they were in a practice match, I would chase the ball or I would fetch water from the canteen and that would make me happy because it made me feel valued to some. I would do it as long as it took to get me in the squad for any games over the weekends so that I can get out of the orphanage, but that never happened. The coach would select the team midweek, and I wouldn't be in it. I could see back then that I would not be the first choice when it comes to the team selection for the games and have never been made any promises that I would ever get to play in any of the matches, but I needed to hold on to something.

One day when I got back to the orphanage from training and was revising in my room for the next day, I had the teacher that introduced me to Peter asking for me. I went to his office, not knowing what it was about. Perhaps I seemed "guilty about something" because whenever I was called, it would be that I had or hasn't done something. This time, however, was very different because the teacher's body language was rather relaxed on the chair behind his desk.

He suggested to me to sit because he had something very important to discuss with me regarding my future. I didn't know which way to take this because every time I was asked to discuss my future, I would get sent somewhere else. I sat uncomfortably, waiting for whatever bad news I might get, ready to leave the room quickly if I was told off. The teacher started the conversation by saying that my mother wished to meet with me, but I stopped listening to him halfway through as my heart was beating fast and my breath became hard to take. The excitement got into me, and all I could think was that my mother, the woman that gave birth to me, has agreed to meet me. The teacher had found her through the phonebook and told her that I was staying in the orphanage. My mother had arranged with him the day and place for us to meet, that is, if I wanted to meet with her. My conversation had finished with the teacher, and it left me almost hysterically happy with the news. I had all sorts of visions of how I would be reunited with my mother and how she would have me back with her family. I shared this with nobody but Ivan since I have considered him to be my boyfriend at the time. The place of our meeting was in the gardens of the football stadium Traikov, the place where I traveled three or four times a week for my training. Can you believe it?

It was shortly before the summer of 1989 when I first met my mother, and I was only fifteen years old. She was accompanied by her son whose name was Ivan, just like my boyfriend, and who also knew little, if anything at all, about who I was to him. He would've been about nine or ten and had a dog that he was holding by the strap, and I noticed when he was given a sign by my mother to go and play away while she and I had some privacy. She was nervous as well, knowing that she could be spotted by neighbors and friends with me, and that it would raise some eyebrows and heads turn with disapproval. In the end, we ignored all passing people and got comfortable on the bench. We were not sitting far from each other, and that gave me the opportunity to study her face while she was talking.

She was saying all sorts, such as how much she wished she had never given me up for adoption and had even tried to find me when I was four years old and how she failed to do so. She then moved on with her life and she was happy to have Ivan and how he was her whole world and she wouldn't want to lose him. Later, she explained that she couldn't afford for her current husband to find out about me because that would break his heart and probably lead to divorce and him taking her son away. She wanted me to promise that I would never ever try to contact her no matter what and to move on with my own life for good. I was very disappointed to learn that I had no place in her life and that I had no meaning to her as a daughter, and so I had only one thing to do. I had to ask the question that she and only she could answer. I needed to know who my father was and how to locate him.

She had a very concerned expression when I asked about him; it was like she was hoping I would never ask. She took a while and then tears started running down her face and she started fighting whatever was making her grieve. She knew I wasn't going to go without the name, and she would have to eventually surrender his name. Before she did, she told me how much she loved him and she was devastated when he died. I thought back then that she was telling me he had died so that I would give up looking for him. I knew it was painful for her to go through memories of a man that had died, and I insisted that I could still contact any of his relatives and that they might find a place for me in their family. She knew I was talking sense and that could be true, so she finally gave away his name and asked me not to involve her in anything. I promised again, and that was how we ended our meeting.

When I got back at the orphanage, some days later the teacher asked me about how the meeting with my mother was and if I was going to remain in touch with her. I explained to him that she had a family of her own and that I had no place in it. I did mention the name of the man who was supposed to be my father and who had died when I was only five years old. He couldn't hide the surprise on his face after I mentioned the name. He slid behind his desk and looked at me with the concerned face of a person who had a puzzle to solve and didn't know from where to start. He picked up the phone and spoke with someone as I was just sitting and paying no attention to his conversation. I was still thinking about the meeting with my mother and had a great feeling to know that she only lives a few blocks from where I was training, and even though I promised not to look for her again, that feeling to see her again was giving me sweet pleasure of possible encounter with her in the future. The teacher had finished with his conversation and was looking at me with a face that had almost found a small resolution of whatever made his face concerned before. He gave me a piece of paper that had an address on it and the name of a person that I had to contact and who would help me with the search of my father's family.

The search for my father's family wasn't as easy as I had imagined it to be. It started with me visiting the consul at the Congo embassy in Pliska. I gave him the same information I had on my father, and he promised to write a letter to the embassy in Moscow on my behalf. He was going to contact me back if he had any news. With this promise, I left his office and focused my attention on school and football in the next few weeks. I had shared all this with my boyfriend Ivan at the time plus my concerns with the coming summer holiday and where I was going to stay for the next two months from July until September. I knew it wasn't his responsibility to help me, but he was the only one I could ask to maybe help me. Finding a place for the summer wasn't my only concern; I also had to be careful where I was traveling during the day and make sure I was surrounded by people because the streets in Pliska were not safe for me any longer. There was a group of mixed-age boys and girls who called themselves "skinheads" and who would attack any minority group in the country, including black people. It was the beginning of the Democratic revolution in the country, and I was in the middle of it.

My teachers at the orphanage were at least concerned for my safety. It was up to me to find a place to stay and food to survive on, and when the time came, they locked the door at the orphanage on me with my bag walking to Ivan's house. He wasn't there, so I left a note on where to find me. I went to Student Town next, knowing that there I can be safe and find food and shelter. Peter was there, and he was very supportive. He arranged for me to stay in a friend's room while he was in England for summer work. The problem of eating was also solved in no matter of time. I simply just went to the students' restaurant, and all I had to do was queue for a meal like every student did. They asked me only the room number where I stayed, and nobody asked me any further questions. There might have been one or two eyebrows raised with suspicion of my age by the staff, but nobody dared to ask. I was told by Peter not to talk with anybody who became curious about me. I have to say that what helped me avoid being caught was my appearance; I was not much different from the African students and easily passed as one of them, not to mention that for the African students I was a new face on the horizon and they all became curious of me.

During the day, I would go to the stadium in Student Town and watch for hours the students playing different games. I would do that almost every day until late in the afternoon. I was hoping that I might get invited to play or even find friends. I had to make sure I never missed the dinner in the student canteen because once the dinner was finished, it was finished and there wasn't more and not that I have never missed a meal. Sometimes at weekends I would get invited by Peter to join him at a party organized by a fellow countryman. The parties would be full with hundreds of African students from not only Nigeria, where Peter came from, but countries like Ethiopia, Ghana, Kenya, Tanzania, and so many more and that even included my father's country.

To my surprise, the first African boy I was introduced to was from same region as my father, and he was no more than a few years older than me. I think Peter intentionally did this so that I could get to mix with people from my fatherland and also help me in the search of my father's family, for which I was very grateful to him. So this boy that I met was named Arthur; he was well mannered and got me dancing to "Eternal Flame" by the Bangles and asked me questions to which I found hard to focus answering because almost everyone in the room was staring at me or had some gossip that involved me or I could've also been just imagining. When the music stopped, Arthur asked me to follow him out so that we could talk in fresh air and away from everyone. I followed him out and in my mind felt sure he wouldn't do anything to me as Peter was there with his wife and knew I was in the hands of this young man from my father's country.

We stopped at a bench and sat down. Arthur was intrigued by me, and that was well shown on his face. He couldn't believe that my father abandoned me just like that in Bulgaria. I could see also the sorrow in his eyes, and then he stretched his arm behind me and pulled me toward him to kiss me. I reacted so furiously to that and slapped him right across his face and made my way back to the party room. To my surprise, Peter was standing not very far from us and must have seen the whole episode, but he didn't say anything after that. Days later, I decided to go to the embassy of Congo and meet with the consul regarding any news on my father's family. The result was negative because he had gone on a summer holiday and had somebody replacing him who didn't know what I was talking about.

On the way back to Student Town, I faced the scare of my life on a bus. It must have been already late out there for them to be around. About a dozen of them were jumping in from every door inside the bus with shaved heads and some tattoos with fascist signs on their arms. I was spotted immediately, and in a few seconds was surrounded. I knew screaming wouldn't help but would only make the situation worse, and trying to get away would make it worse too so I just sat there quietly. The leader of the group made his way through the bodies of skinheads, and the first thing I saw was his black boots and army trousers. He stopped and had a little stare at me before announcing to the others to leave me alone because I was "colored." My heart was pumping fast from the close encounter with the skinheads, and I knew that if I'd get away with it, it was only for now. The skinhead boys moved to the front area of the bus where they sat, some of their eyes still on me. Surely some of them were disappointed that I got away with it and probably I would have been perfect for the ones who had never done it before. I have read in some articles that in Germany and especially the eastern part of the country, many foreign people have suffered from the hands of the so-called skinheads. Some never made it alive, and here I was sitting next to a dozen of them going in the same direction to Student Town. I had sympathy with the foreign people and how hard it must be for them, being sent by their governments to study in a country that was peaceful until they showed up, the skinheads.

The revolution in Eastern Europe began, and almost every country recorded cases of attacks against foreign citizens. Todor Zhivkov, the president at the time, probably knew his days were numbered and people were marching on the streets with slogans "Communists out" and all sorts. This wasn't my fight, and I tried not to get involved in the protests that led to the headquarters of state. However, I couldn't dismiss the excitement that people were going through at the time, and the skinheads saw the opportunity to join in the fight of liberation of Bulgaria. Now Student Town was the main target for the crimes, and even though they had a police station there, the police did almost nothing to keep the people safe from what was coming. I heard one African student telling someone that the police were corrupt and some of the police officers demanded the African students to pay them money in order to protect them, and yet the Student Town was for me the safest place to be. The skinheads on the bus were going there, and they wanted someone's blood. Some of them even carried knives and were half drunk already. They got off on the first stop in Student Town.

I continued on the bus relieved that nothing bad happened to me and had to warn Peter of the band. I couldn't go myself to the police because I didn't want to uncover the reason what I was doing in the town. I was only fifteen, had no personal identification yet, and knew that I could be held at the station just for that. Peter was pleased that I was unharmed and safe, but not happy that skinheads were in town. He, however, did nothing that I would have expected him to do, like call the police or at least warn them. I had sympathy for him too. I know he put his family first, and that was something I didn't understand because I never had one.

On the following day, we went to the canteen for breakfast and then learned that the skinheads had attacked one of the African students with knives and he was fighting for his life at the emergency room. That news spread a shock among the people in Student Town and mainly the foreign students. People were prepared to fight back, and some went to buy knives for their own protection. The African students became united with each day and would start moving in groups, which did help a bit, but the police received warnings from the locals that they were scared to be out because the "Negroes" were in packs everywhere and they believed something dodgy was going on. The police would enter into conflict with the Africans and arrest them. Sometimes they would have someone arrested just to show the others what would happen to them as a warning.

My summer holiday was coming to an end as we were in September. I thanked Peter for helping me out with a place to stay and promised to continue contact. Back in the orphanage, all was a bit depressing for me with white people everywhere and I couldn't help feeling different, making my life even harder. Don't get me wrong; I am not being racist. After all, I was born to think as white. I was born to act white, but the problem was I didn't want to think like white. I wanted to be me and be happy for who I am.

The months rolled by as I did the same thing over and over, from school to playing football and then the orphanage. Still not allowed to play in the team on the weekends, I was left with no choice but to leave the club in search of my father's family, an adventure that completely took over me and my life. I have dedicated myself to discovering my roots, with or without my mother's help. I was sixteen years old in 1990 and started to feel more comfortable with my race and, as a matter of fact, felt proud of being black. The music of Whitney Houston and Michael Jackson fueled me with more inspiration; I had the cassettes from Peter. I still didn't have many friends and that was hard, but I wouldn't dwell too much on that.

My boyfriend Ivan and I would see each other occasionally, but there was tension around him whenever we would get to be alone. He wanted more from me, and I wasn't ready. Then we went for months not seeing each other for which I didn't blame myself too much. I had received some anticipating news that came to me via a letter sent to the orphanage. It was sent by the students' president of my father country, and he was notifying me of the ambassador's visit to Bulgaria and that a party was to be held in his honor that same weekend. The news was shockingly happy for me, as I was hoping for an end to my current life and a new beginning. I waited almost a whole week for the party, and when the time came, I was there. Everyone else was dressed very smartly for the occasion, and I only had a sports suit and trainers to wear, not that I was much into dressing, but it made me feel uncomfortable. From the judgement I made, the people were mainly from my father country, students or people from other African nations that played some importance. I knew a few people from Student Town already, but however they felt about my dress I would quickly blend with the crowd as though I hadn't noticed them.

I finally got to Fernando, the person responsible for sending me the invitation; and wasting no time, I found myself queuing to meet the ambassador who was surrounded by people. In fact, it didn't look like I had a chance to get near him. He was an old man, very old, who was looking at me over his glasses that were hanging over his nose. He invited me with a gesture to join him at his table that was covered with bottles and cocktail glasses. I was offered a drink and had to refuse since I wasn't drinking. He had a long look at me, and the same went for me. I had to consider that he didn't speak Bulgarian, I did not understand Portuguese, yet I could try Russian, which I had a basic knowledge of. However, Fernando offered to be translator in this case, and I couldn't refuse.

So I got started by introducing myself and giving the name of my father to the ambassador, who at first certainly wasn't much interested to what I was saying until I mentioned the name of my father, which made him move in his chair uncomfortably. Fernando himself felt uncomfortable next to me, and I continued with the story of my mother and father, of how they both met. Of course, with the shocked faces of the ambassador and Fernando, I stopped talking for a second, feeling that I must have said something wrong!

There was silence at the table for a few seconds, and at the end it was the ambassador who broke the silence. "You are saying that our former president of state was your father?"

It was my turn to look shocked and speechless. I had no idea what had happened, and I said, "I swear, never did I mention he was a president and my mother never said he was." In my moment of shock, I was asked to leave the party immediately. Part of me wanted to fight back, not to let be pushed out just because of some comment I have just made, but I couldn't.

Everyone was already staring at me with eyes that were almost sending me to execution for spoiling their party night. I found my way out of the restaurant in the dark, where I stood for a few minutes trying to digest what had just happened. My father was a president, and my mother skipped this important detail from me. I felt humiliation and anger that I had not known who my father really was and that if he was the president, why the hell was I living in an orphanage? Why was I abandoned? I knew that only one person could answer this question, and that was my mother. I know I had promised her not to contact her again, but this news was of great importance to my life and I needed to know more about my father. I have to say the news of my father being former president of state didn't flatter me one bit. If anything, I was angry that he didn't do something about me and never tried to look for me. There was lots of "ifs" and "buts," even "maybe" he didn't know about me, and this was why I had to see my mother again.

I phoned her, and she was okay at first when she answered the phone. As I went on telling her that I learned about my father and his position in life, she went mental and shouted down the line to never ever speak about him to her, followed by a big smash on the phone and the line going dead. I left her alone for the next few months because I felt bad for her and her family, as she had said "if my husband finds out." I haven't been happy since learning my father was president, and it would be difficult to contact the embassy in Moscow after what happened in the restaurant. I saw my father being a president as a barrier to my happiness and a big obstacle to connect with my relatives in Africa. I knew my task to connect with my family was getting even harder, and the desperation of not knowing what to do pushed me to Student Town again, this time not to see Peter but to find and learn more about my father's culture with people from his country. That was how my life in Student Town turned to be a visit almost every day after school.

I met a woman called Nazare or "Nana." She was from Angola, more or less four years older than me. She liked me very much as a friend as I did her. We became close friends, and I even considered her as a sister. She introduced me to my community in Pliska at occasions, like parties often held by the students themselves. Later, my friend Peter learned from someone that I had been visiting Student Town often without visiting him, for which I was guilty, and that put an end to our friendship. I was sad, of course, because he was the first African I had contact with. I learned that the Africans from my father's country didn't get on with the Nigerians and the Zulandans for some awkward reasons with their African history. So for instance, I was accepted in the community as one of them and I was seen with other African nation members, it wasn't good in the eyes of the others. And for that matter, I was asked once by Nana if I had a boyfriend, and when she and her friends learned he was Bulgarian, that didn't go down well either. They made fun of me and protested against the idea of me being with a white man. I was introduced to many nice-looking men from my fatherland, and a few have caught my eye, I have to admit. But they either had a girlfriend or were one of those who didn't speak proper Bulgarian. Being friends with Nana had minuses as well, as she was considered by the fellow men as a very loose woman, not that I had any problem with that; but rumors that I was becoming one came as a shock to me. I had to reconsider our friendship, and without saying much to her, I kind of distanced myself and she didn't react very well to that because everyone from my father country had been told that I had stolen her stereo and also that I had been trying to sleep with her boyfriend behind her back. Of course, none of that was true, but it was too late and did damage me for a while. I stopped going to Student Town and focused on school and the few months left before the summer.

Ivan and I reestablished our relationship and were seeing each other almost every night before the door to the orphanage was locked. My feelings for him were growing every day, and his desire to have me just as much. The fact that I wasn't ready to be with him led to problems, such as his starting to see other women, mainly his ex. I found it hard to believe when one of the boys came to me while I was reading my book in my room and said that he had seen my boyfriend with another girl in the cafeteria in the town center. I didn't believe it and yet jumped to my feet to go and see for myself, and it was all true. He was with a woman around his age with his arms around her back, chilling out with a glass of vodka and tonic. As he saw me, I would have expected him to react defensively or even deny any wrongdoing, but he didn't. I left immediately because I didn't know what else to do and hoped that he would follow me out, but he didn't. I was falling into pieces. I loved that man and I swore he showed me that he loved me too, so what was the problem between us? I had to get him out of my head because he wasn't worth it anymore, and it was hard to imagine him with another woman.

As weeks turned into months, I was back on the streets for the summer holiday. The orphanage closed its doors behind my back, and I just followed the unknown. I was sixteen years old with just a few clothes on my back and without money. I had to figure out where to go for the remaining two and a half months. Ivan and I hadn't seen each other since I saw him with his ex, and I didn't think I really wanted to see him. I could have gone to Peter in Student Town, but the problem was we had stopped talking, and my going to Student after last been accused of stealing wasn't a good idea. I was a very proud person, and knowing that someone has a low opinion about me, I just stop seeing that person full stop. I had no other choice but to go to the train station where the trains to Preslavo depart, and maybe if I got onto the train unnoticed, I could go to the place where I grew up. So I followed my initial thought and went to the train station. It was as big as I last remembered it when I was a child. We used to wait with our bags for the train to arrive for hours. If I could only go back in time when I was happy and not have to worry about where to sleep or what to eat during my holidays. I was too young to even consider looking for a job that would've helped. There wasn't much room for sentimental feelings. I was at the train station and had to look for a comfortable place to wait or even sleep. Wherever I looked, there were people rushing around with luggage, and I was kind of standing in the middle, not knowing which way to go. So I followed the smell of fresh soup that was coming from the upstairs floor at the station; being up there would also give me a better view of the whole station.

I had already noticed the uniformed officers who were armed and stopping here and there to check passports or to give any information to some lost passenger. I found a table where there were some leftovers, and I sat there, pretending it was I who bought the food. Remembering that people were coming and asking to sit on the table since there were three available seats and after that someone would come to clear the table, I had to pretend to have a drink and food or else I would've been kicked out. People were coming and going, and I was still sitting there, not knowing where to go. As it was getting darker outside and the staff were rushing to close and go to their homes, I had to start moving. I had a whole day to observe that some people were sleeping on the benches or others were just sitting and reading a newspaper undisturbed by anyone, I thought this was ideal for me. I had some books in my bag and a pair of underwear, socks, T-shirt, and a sweater. My bag wasn't big, so I couldn't fit in much anyway.

I found this comfortable place to sit with a near view to the window where I could watch all the taxis coming and going. I used my bag as a pillow and covered my feet with my sweater, and that was how I fell asleep my first night at the train station. It wasn't a very comfortable sleep like in the orphanage because of the light and the music that was coming through the speakers, but I was tired.

The following morning, I was woken up by the loud station announcer. I noticed that most of the people sitting opposite me had nothing else to do but stare at me. Some thought that I had missed the last night's train and this was why I had slept on the bench. Others, I guess, thought that I might be homeless and whispering along that maybe they should call someone. It was unacceptable that I was sleeping on a bench that was made for sitting; others were whispering like I couldn't hear them. I had to make my move. I had to go somewhere else, a different corner or something. I didn't like to be in people's sight for long because that could only lead to trouble—one thing that I learned when I was in the orphanage in Preslavo. I started walking around, something like exploring the station. I needed to know where the toilets were and stopped on many occasions looking at the information board with the timetables of the trains. I was looking for Preslavo in particular, not that I was convinced that I should go there, also having to know that the children there will be more likely to have been sent away for the summer holiday and the orphanage itself will be closed.

I knew almost everyone in the village there, but would any one of them want me in their house for the summer and provide me with free meal and roof? I bet the people in Preslavo thought that I was well looked after in Pliska and had a place to stay and food to eat, and indeed since I have been in Pliska, nobody came to visit me to see if I was okay. No, things have changed for me and I had to stay put together in Pliska. I had things to deal with, like finding a way to convince my mother to help me with the search of my father's family. To get to her house was a challenge itself. I didn't know the routes in Pliska that well and had no idea of the quickest way to her house from the train station. I had no money with me to even try to call her from the pay phone at the station, which they had everywhere. So I made my decision to go and visit her no matter what and how angry that would make her.

With a bit of asking here and there, I got to her neighborhood, and it was probably around lunchtime when I was at the front door of her apartment and was ringing the doorbell. At first, I thought that nobody was in there, then I heard a little boy's voice and knew that it had to be my little brother Ivan. I could hear the footsteps closing near the door as the peephole on the door was covered with shadow. I knew my mother knew it was me, and I asked to speak with her. What came next was something I wasn't prepared for and took me by surprise. She opened the door almost instantly, and she was holding a big thick stick, like one of those used for preparing bread. Anyway, she had it in her right hand and she looked so furious and asked me to leave nicely, but I wanted to ask her a few more questions about my father. I had made the journey all the way to her house, and I didn't want to upset her or anything. I knew she wasn't going to use this stick on me, but I was wrong! She waved it in front of my face and then hit me on the head.

I stepped backward and didn't even try to protect myself as she hit me again through my body, shouting at the same time words like "ugly monkey" and "black cockroach." Her hitting me wasn't what tore my heart to pieces that day but her words. Standing in front of me wasn't the woman who gave birth to me, the woman that I loved through the years despite not knowing her. The same woman that I have forgiven for giving me up for adoption and I loved despite all the pain she had caused me. I knew I wasn't right to be there at her house with her son watching the scene of violence. I felt that I wouldn't hate her even after that and I would never hurt her. One of the neighbors was running toward her, trying to stop her from hurting me, and all I could hear was "Get rid of this bastard!" My mother was screaming hysterically. I left the building heartbroken, with tears of pain that I had lost my mother again. Perhaps deep inside me I was hoping that maybe one day she would love me, and now that day would never come.

I was wandering the streets and with an empty stomach, not that I was even thinking about food. I just didn't care anymore. It was as though the life was sucked out of me. She made me feel like nothing, something even lower than a cockroach, and the term *black* that she used completely described me. I didn't choose to be born in this country. I had the right to know who my father was. She had no right to keep him away from me, and if I was black to her, why the hell did she continue sleeping with black men? I went back to the train station and needed to find something to eat, even if it was something from the floor. I was hungry and needed my energy.

The first place I went to was the restaurant, and I got lucky in a way because there was a woman with a girl of mixed race, just like me. It's like God had sent them there. The girl was approximately my age and was happy when she saw me, and that was when her mother noticed me. I kind of pretended not to have seen them and sat on a table that wasn't clean yet, hoping to find something else on the plates before somebody came. I knew I was being watched by the woman and the girl, and I was wondering what they were thinking of me. I have to say that at this point, I didn't care how I looked or if my hair was in order. I know I probably smelled a bit, but to me, that was normal considering my circumstances. I haven't used a shower for days, and I know that if I wished to, I could go to Ivan's place and ask to have a shower, but my dignity was in the way and especially of what happened when I last saw him. So as I was sitting, the mother of the mixed-race girl came to my table and invited me to join them. I was so excited and couldn't refuse the offer, and yet at the same time I didn't want to show any emotion. I followed her and sat next to the girl, who was introduced to me as Victoria and the mother's name as Tania.

Her mother asked me if I was alone, and my first instinct was not to expose myself; after all, I didn't know this woman. I lied and said that I was waiting for someone. She, I would reckon, didn't accept what I said and continued with all sorts of questions, like she was trying to get to the bottom of my story. Her daughter Victoria was quiet, and all she did was smile at me each time I looked at her. I have to say just having some attention from these two made me feel a bit better. Then came a big African man to our table and gave a big hug to the mother and then Victoria. He was the one they were waiting to arrive from Plovdiv, the second largest city in Bulgaria. I was introduced to him, and he offered everyone a drink; and if I had an opportunity to walk away, it was then. I was nobody to them and didn't even know this people, but I didn't walk away; I stayed. I had food and a drink for which I had to thank almost every time. I took a bite from the sandwich. I knew this wouldn't last forever and was thankful for the moment that somebody shared with me.

When the time came to leave, I was stopped by Tania. "Do you have a place to go?" I couldn't lie and just shook my head in response, as I felt embarrassed about lying to her previously. She hugged me and said, "Great, you are coming with us! We have a spare bed for you at home, don't we, Vicky?"

Next, we were in the taxi driving us to her apartment. I have to say I was still a bit unsure if I was making the right decision by letting myself into a stranger's hands. The comfort was having Vicky next to me as assurance that nothing would happen to me. Still having the fresh memories of the encounter with my mother in my head, I thought that if I was a "black cockroach" to her, what would I be to others? However, I needed to have faith in the good and in people; not all of them were like my mother, and besides, it's only for one night and then I would think of something else.

The apartment wasn't very big, but it had enough space for all of us. It had two bedrooms and a bath, with a dining room and TV. I was shown where to sleep and offered a shower and some pajamas that belonged to Vicky's sister who had moved to live with her father in France some years back. I learned from Vicky that her mom had four other children and they had all been given to orphanages. I felt uncomfortable with that news since I was one of those children, also left by my mother. However, Vicky said her mother had intentions to have them back one day when she could afford them, and that was only if she wins the battle with the local council for a bigger bedroom apartment.

Anyway, after my shower, Tania came to the room to see if I was comfortable and to make sure Vicky and I were getting along well. She suggested that we all spend a day in tomorrow and watch movies, so I guess that meant I wasn't going anywhere and I was happy with that too. The evening went smoothly and Vicky and I went to bed, and I don't know about her, but I wasted no time for sleep. The next day, breakfast was served, and we were still wearing pajamas as Vicky and me sat to eat. Tania was putting laundry away and asking from a distance if everything was okay with the breakfast and if we wanted some more toast. I was good with what I had in front of me and ate everything. I had no place else to be but there, with them watching movies, and even if I wanted to go, I couldn't because Tania had my clothes washed and they were hanging on the balcony.

Hours later, we all got relaxed on the sofas and were watching TV when Tania wanted to know more about me and where I lived and if there was someone who would be worried about me. I owed her the truth for giving me food and roof over my head. I told her everything about me, from the life in the kindergarten to the boarding school in Pavlovo. I told her I had no place to stay during the holidays and that I really hoped to find my father's family. She asked me if I knew anything about my mother, and I told her that she didn't want anything to do with me. I didn't tell her about the last meeting I had with her because I partly blamed myself for what happened. When I told her my mother's name, she became silent, went out of the room, and then came back silently with a big photo album. She started turning the pages until she stopped where she wanted to and passed it to me. I looked at the photograph carefully, and Tania said, "This is your mother," pointing at a young blond woman who looked happy and somewhere in her early twenties. Tania was there too on that picture; they were sitting next to African men who were holding glasses up in some kind of toast, celebrating something. Tania said that she knew my mother back from the early seventies and that she was dating people from my father's country mainly while Tania was dating men from Nigeria.

She told me that back then it was very hard for white women to be seen out with black men and that she was one of the few who wasn't embarrassed to be seen with them. She said that my mother was a bitch back then, and she wasn't surprised that she left me for adoption. What did puzzle Tania was the time I was born. She swore that I surely had my birth certificate mixed up because she remembered my mother being pregnant in 1971, and that was the time she was hanging out with her at pubs or parties, which Africans would attend. I was confused just as much to learn the story of their lives back then and from the way she was saying it. It seemed as though my mother liked being with black people until something changed. Anyway, I asked Tania if I could keep the photograph of my mother, and she said there was no need to ask as she was going to give it to me anyway. She didn't keep in contact with my mother since she got married to a white man. I was really touched to have a picture of my mother, and for the next few days, I kept it so close to me at all times. I stayed a few more days at Tania's and then decided that it was time for me to move on. I had other things on my mind, such as finding a way to contact my father's family, and the way for me to do it was to find someone to write a letter in Portuguese and help me send it to the embassy based in Moscow. I didn't know how well my presence at Student Town would go down with the others and especially the Angolan community after having claimed to be the daughter of a late president.

I could have gone to visit Peter, but I felt like I had betrayed him by going to other African students and if not ashamed of doing that. I would have expected him of all others to understand my motives behind that and how important his help could have been to me. Nana, on the other hand, I knew I couldn't trust, and I also needed to clarify with her the accusation against me. So I went to find her in her apartment and asked to speak with her at the reception, and they just let me go through. She was in her room, and after seeing me through the peephole, she opened the door with a smile like nothing had ever happened. I pretended not to have noticed her smile and walked into her room. She offered me a drink, which I accepted, and then she apologized for blaming me for stealing her stereo, which she had found days later in one of her friends' room. How her stereo got in someone else's room, I never asked. It was just a relief to know she had found it and she knew it wasn't me who stole it. Great! That meant that she had no bad feelings toward me and we could still be friends.

Nana and I became even closer than before, something more like sisters I could say. She started dressing me in her clothes, which were nice too. She became responsible for my hair every day or she felt she was, and I don't know how, but she managed to convince the people at the reception that I was her relative who was staying for a while. So I had it all going for me then—food, nice bed, hot water, even Nana herself wrote and sent a letter to the embassy on my behalf. I would be with her everywhere she went and even one day took me to watch a football match between the students. My father's countrymen were playing against another African representative, and as we sat to watch the game, I could feel every eye on me. That was the time when I was really kind of introduced to the community, and after the game, which they had obviously won, it was time to party. These people really knew how to have a party, and I was there because I was one of them. They always played loud music with rhythms that could make anyone dance, and they did know how to dance. Often I would see loads of Bulgarian girls invited, but not white guys. In fact, I would never see any other African nationality to their parties. Sometimes someone from Ghana would try to sneak in and then fights would follow and the police would be involved. For me, I always tried to keep my distance.

I have to give it to Nana; she always had me covered in situations like this. She made sure I only consumed free-alcohol drinks, and if she was to go and dance with someone, she always had her eye on me. Whenever she did turn her back, someone would try to convince me for a dance or to leave the room with him for a small talk in fresh air. Often they would stink of alcohol and I didn't need Nana to tell me that it's not a good company for me. You see, in their heads I was a woman, not a sixteen-year-old girl, and Nana did warn me that most of them would just want to sleep with me and that's it. She explained to me that the men from my father's country living in Europe were not good because they'd been spoiled with money, which the government sends them every year, and they drown themselves in alcohol. Most women catching those men for the money would be some loose Bulgarian women, which an ordinary Bulgarian man wouldn't look twice. Of course, there were a few of them who would have a nice-looking woman with proper behavior and she would be respected among the rest of the community; but of course, that type of woman wasn't allowed to join in such parties. Nana knew she would have a very hard job on her hands to protect me from those people, and she decided to introduce me to someone whom she had faith would protect me. His name was Jose, first-year student from my father's country and well behaved too. Nana trusted him and I trusted him too eventually, and it's not like I would spend my days with him because I didn't, but he was there for me like a shoulder in need. My summer was coming to an end, and I had to go back to the boarding school. Things were looking much brighter for me in a way that I had created a friendship with people from my father's country and I had something to hold on to, a belief that one day I would go home to Africa.

I resumed school in September 1990, and all was back to normal, until I found that sign on my desk with the Nazi cross. The teachers got involved in the investigation, and weeks went by with nobody to blame after that. I tried to pretend that nothing happened and that it was only a joke, but it wasn't. The attitude at class toward me was different, and if some of my classmates used to talk to me at class, they had stopped. I never tried to ask what was the problem because deep down, I knew the problem was my skin, and I really didn't belong there. I had incidents where someone would spit on me while I was sitting at my desk, someone that I would help in the past with homework, and I wouldn't say a word of complaint when the teacher walked into the room. What we had then was an attitude flamed by the political instability in the country, and it was shown in the teenagers. Some of them thought it was cool being "free" as democratic behavior was conducted through youngsters in the country, believing that it would go unpunished. However, it was going to be my word against theirs.

I became more and more vulnerable to them, and they knew it. During the breaks of fifteen minutes, I wouldn't dare go outside in the school yard as previously, knowing that young skinheads from the neighborhood knew of me and were waiting for me to go out on my break. Skinhead signs would appear on walls outside the school, declaring their territory, and none of the teachers would even bother trying to remove it because they would appear again and again. I had a time when I didn't show up for school and nobody cared a bit; it was like I was one less problem to deal with. The culmination was coming, and one day when I was just about to enter the door to the school, I was grabbed from behind and pulled to the ground. About four or five of them started kicking me as I was trying to cover my face. People were waiting on the side for their transport, and nobody dared to get involved. Then from somewhere, I had the strength to get up while still being punched everywhere and hit one of them back in the face.

The reaction took him by surprise, and the rest stepped aside to watch a fight between a black girl and a white boy. Never ever to that point in my life had I fought back for being racially abused. I was strong and stubborn, knowing I was going to lose the fight, but I wouldn't give up. In the end, a teacher ran up along, shouting for everyone to return to their classrooms, for me to go and clean up myself and then the director's office. I was in his office minutes later, still probably bleeding from my bruises, and explained what had happened; but that didn't matter. I was sent back to the boarding school with suspension. I was supposed to have been a threat to the other children at school or something like that, and a letter was sent to the director of the boarding school explaining the reasons for my suspension. My self-esteem was really low, and I was desperate to be liked and feel close to someone that had pushed me to my mother's area. But that was the last place for me to be after the argument, yet in a weird way, I felt safe there. It was supposed to be one night, but then they turned into many and the more I was there, the more I wanted to be there. What I did was start waiting until dusk and then sit on a bench that was distanced like a hundred meters from my mother's apartment but with a view to her apartment.

I started watching her when she came from work or shopping and my little brother Ivan around her playing while she was unloading things from the car. I would imagine that I was there next to her and felt her love, like the one she was showing my brother. I never judged her, and all I did was admire her, the way she carried herself. She wouldn't know I was sitting there, and I always made sure I wasn't there for too long. Sometimes people would sit on the bench next to me and I would take a walk until they had gone and then would sit there until my mother went inside. Then I would continue sitting there with the hope to see her silhouette through the window and imagine I was there too, and when all the lights had been switched off, I would get inside the building and sleep on the staircase, the same that she walked on every day, for some comfort. I did it until I was caught by one of her neighbors early in the morning as he was leaving for work and he saw me sleeping on the floor. He gave me a push and said he would call the police if I didn't disappear quickly. His voice must have been loud enough because I could see the light coming on below the door of my mother's flat. So that was one place down for me to sleep, and I knew the risk of going back there. I did continue, however, sitting on the bench and watching my mother from a distance, not every day she was there; plus I also stopped because of the snow.

The Christmas holidays were drawing near, and I had yet to find a place to stay during that time. I had no other place to be but the train station; at least I could be safe knowing that skinheads were everywhere and a place like the train station had police patrol. One evening, I had fallen asleep without realizing that a man had sat near me and had me covered with his jacket for warmth. "Nothing wrong with that," people around could have said and probably even me if I was awake, but I wasn't. He had my hand on his thing doing stuff as he only knew. He was touching my back, and that was when I woke up, realizing what was happening. With disgust, I pushed him and his jacket away from me, only to uncover that he had my pants slightly opened. People around must have seen what was happening and did nothing! My initial reaction was to grab my stuff and rush out in the cold.

I wasn't safe there and would have to find a different place to stay for the night of which I had no recollection of the time. I just sat at a bus stop for a while, not knowing what I was going to do and then got on the first bus going nowhere. I just needed to be warm and have a place to sleep, and before I knew it, I was asleep again on the bus. It was the radiator next to me that made me feel so warm and relaxed that I had fallen asleep. I woke up when the bus was in its garage. Garage! Why on earth didn't the driver wake me up at the last stop? I was thinking. Walking toward the front door, knowing he was sitting there on the driver's seat, I asked him to open the door and he refused. He asked me to do something else first before he opened the doors. I refused and started stepping backward to the back of the bus, clinging to the seats. Luckily for me, another bus was arriving at the time and I started shouting as loud as I could. The driver panicked as he saw no other option but to let me go. I was out in the cold in a place I have never been before, and from the looks of it, wherever I was, I would have to stay there until morning.

The garage was quite far from the residential areas, and I was forced to walk all the way while I was covered in snow. Eventually, I got to the residential buildings and started looking for one that had heating on so that I could dry my socks and trainers. A few of the buildings I had tried were locked, and those were the ones that would mainly have heating still on. I continued looking but couldn't find one, so I just settled to sleep on the staircase with one eye open. More or less I had two or three hours of sleep, and that was all I needed before everyone in the building left for work. I got one of the early buses and went to Student Town, a place where the canteen would be open and I could sneak and have breakfast with the students, and after that I would think of something. Most students would have their breakfast and go to lectures until two or three in the afternoon, so basically Student Town would be almost dead during the day. I didn't want to be noticed in the day, so I decided to ride the buses and explore more of Pliska. I had my card from school that entitled me to travel free of charge, and I intended to use it. I went anywhere on the bus from the north part of Pliska to the south and back to the center. I started visiting shops like Levi's many times per day. I liked the jeans and the jackets and just wished I could have them. Some shops I wasn't allowed to go in, I never bothered trying again. I had my routine like every day, and in the evenings I had found a great place to stay until four in the morning. That was the nightclub in Student Town called "Joe." At first when I tried, it was very hard to get in, but there was this mixed-race girl called Nicole who worked there as a waitress. She had felt sorry maybe for me, I don't know, but she knew the guards and they never said a word. I was in and always had a Pepsi on the house, only one per evening. I would just sit there listening to the music and watching people dance.

If I was tired, I just slept on the couch undisturbed, and only when it was time for cleaning I would help and then Nicole would go home and I would wander in Student Town until the canteen opened for breakfast. I had all pretty much going well the way I wanted for me until Ivan showed up. He has been looking for me everywhere since I left the boarding school, and he met this person called Charlie from Kenya, who told him where to find me. So he found me in nightclub Joe and wanted me to go back with him and stay there for the remainder of my holiday. I was happy to know that he cared for me, and then he told me that he had dumped his ex again and how much he missed me. With this, I was already in his arms again. I stayed at his house for a few days unnoticed by his parents because this was something Ivan wanted. Of course, that was something that made me feel uncomfortable, but what other alternative had I? I knew that sooner or later his parents would learn about me, and if he couldn't stand up to defend our relationship, then it was doomed. After all, I didn't choose to hide underneath the bed each time his mother knocked at the door to ask for something or even wait out by the terrace half naked in the cold! He thought he could hide me forever, and when the moment came, he didn't know how to deal with it again.

It was in the early hours of a Saturday morning and his parents had gone out very early to the market to sell their vegetables. We had the house to ourselves, or at least that was what we intended to do. Ivan was making us breakfast when the door to the bedroom opened and there stood his girlfriend. She had let herself in with the spare key she had to the house, obviously given to her by her boyfriend. She started shouting his name and he came right away, and she demanded an explanation from him and he had nothing to say. I couldn't leave anyway because all I had on was pants, and before I even made any move to reach for the rest of my clothes, his ex took them away, with delight on her face. Ivan followed her, trying to convince her to give them back, but she wasn't having it and opened the window wide and, just like that, threw them out on the snow. Then she demanded that I leave the house, and there he stood and did nothing.

It was clear to me that she was still in a relationship with him and he was with her too, or else he would've sent her packing long ago. I was hurt and humiliated for believing him and giving myself to him. The humiliation of going out there and having to dress in front of watching eyes said it all—I was the stupid one, and with time, I might have learned how to avoid the humiliation. I turned my back on him and went back to the boarding school with the hope of starting on better terms at school and try to forget the episode with Ivan and his ex, but it wasn't to be.

He came one night very late to my window and climbed the pipes, holding to the metal gratings that were on the way and straining his muscles. There he was begging me to let him in the room. At that time I was on my own because the other two girls hadn't gotten back from the holidays. He wouldn't have known that, and if I wanted he would have been in; plus he was drunk and drunk as he could ever get. He went on singing my name and almost got me into trouble. You see, he did manage to get the other children's attentions, and some even joined in begging me to let him in and stop the noise he was making. Someone, however, went to the teacher to report and he immediately asked Ivan to leave or he was going to call the police. I wasn't having a laugh, and the following day I wasn't having a laugh at the office of the director when he was partly blaming me for the mockery Ivan made with the teacher. I was now supposed to give his name to the local prosecutor for further investigation, and information on where he lived would be greatly appreciated. Only that I wasn't that kind of person. I knew he had his faults, and after what he did, he probably deserved that. But he didn't do any harm to anyone. I couldn't do it and denied knowing anything about him. I did say he knew my name through someone I might know and had to convince them that I didn't invite him to my window after midnight.

Eventually I had to be released from the director's office as he saw it as a complete waste of time, and he only warned me that if this happened again I would be suspended from the boarding school, not that I would have much control of that. Ivan, for my utmost luck, didn't show up for the next few days and believe me what a relief it had been for me. But little did I know that other problems I would have with him would completely change the course of my life. I resumed my lessons, and we were in January 1991, a year full of promise and two years left of my school. I was yet to hear anything from the embassy on my letter that I have sent months ago via Nana, and it was getting to me. Some inner voice was telling me that the people at the embassy would not answer me because they had already dismissed my claims through the ambassador when he was last in Bulgaria. I was going to give up for that matter either, if not encouraging me to continue. I hadn't seen my mother or even been anywhere near her place, but I had her picture with me everywhere I went. I had given up on her to help me in any way, and I wasn't intending to enlist her help. I mean, the woman knew where to find me if she wanted to and never tried. She had no scruples for leaving me behind in the hands of the government, also knowing the current environment in the country and the dangers I would be facing, not that I have mentioned any of this to her. She had it all sorted for herself and her family. Married to a white guy and having a son with whom she played happy family, give me a break! I honestly don't bite for a second that there isn't a day in her life since she met with me that she doesn't ask herself the question, I wonder how she is. And I wanted to believe in that. It gave me hope that one day maybe she would change her tune and finally I would hear her saying the stuff I wanted to hear, but that day was far away and maybe would never come.

I stayed out of any provocations at school, and I almost never had the teacher's eyes on me, which was good for the reason that during breaks I could go outside in the yard and sit on a bench knowing that they couldn't do anything to me. I was being monitored for my own safety and kind of liked that, yet when out of school, I was on my own. I avoided the town center, which meant me taking the tram that would lead to a station that had turned into one of the meeting points of the skinheads. So instead of going that way, I was taking the tram in the opposite direction that would take me an hour more to get to the boarding school and more changing transport. The bus that I would normally first take was the same bus but going in the opposite direction to the boarding school and would take me to Student Town, and this was where I went on one of the sunny spring days after school.

Heading straight to Nana's apartment to learn of any news on my letter, I couldn't find Nana in her room, so I went directly to Jose's place and he was there. He invited me in and offered tea, and while he was preparing my tea, I had my attention on a picture he had on his wall. It was the man himself on the photograph, my father, the late president of his country. I asked Jose if that was him, and he said yes. Over the cup of tea we talked, or more like he talked about the person on the picture and how, thanks to him, his country was free and students like Jose were able to travel to another country and study. Jose was just as excited to know that the man on the photo was my father but that he knew nothing of my existence. He then kind of felt like it was his duty to show me pictures of my father and went to grab his country history book. I wasn't sure what I was going to see there, but he suggested I better have a look at the pictures. I took the book with trembling hands and nervously opened the first page.

It was all written in Portuguese, and I wasn't even trying to read; I was looking for that first picture of my father to appear. Then I saw him standing in front of a microphone like he was giving a speech and he was surrounded by people, and my eyes watered at his image. I couldn't take my eyes off it. Jose said there were more pictures to see, and I saw them all and left the book aside to go and clear my face of sorrow to a man I have never met—a man whom I would never get to meet and call Dad. It was all too much and I never thought it would hurt so much, but it did. Jose did mention the resemblance I had with my father, which was unmistakable, and he promised to help me with my cause. First thing he was going to do was write a letter to his brother, who was a lawyer, back home and explain all the details and send pictures of me, and second, he was going to write to the president's office and all I had to do was wait.

I had nothing else but trust Jose with this. I promised not to talk with anyone else about this, even Nana, and we stayed in touch via mail. Of course, I wasn't intending to jeopardize Jose's life after the way he put it into words. He told me that the government had been fighting with the opposition party for a decade and the two parties had agreed to hold the first presidential elections ever in 1992, and story of this character could be seen as damaging to the image of the ruling party. Also, since Jose was sent by the current government to study in Bulgaria, he wanted to see his graduation through without any problem, which I totally understood. I later visited Nana's apartment, and she was happy to see me after a long time and never mentioned a word about Jose. Nana loved cooking at her flat, and she was one of the very few I knew to do that. Most students would be at the canteen, but not Nana. She knew how to cook rice with chicken covered in a lovely sauce, which was just as delicious for me as anything else. We watched one of the new movies that had come out on video, *Pretty Woman* with Julia Roberts, and I remember thinking at the end, "I so hope something nice happens to me at the end too."

Easter holiday, I was at Tania's and her daughter Victoria. They were busy as ever preparing home-baked cake and decorating eggs, something I enjoyed doing. We all went to pick our eggs from the local market, and there were queues of people waiting since the early hours of the morning to get to the best eggs. Tania was considerably big in size and wasn't one of those whom you would like to mess about. Some people were looking at us with obscenity, like being second-class citizens, but Tania didn't care about their opinion as we got what we came for and left the spotlight. After all the food was dished up, we had to wait for a friend of Tania's to arrive. Tania mentioned that this friend was also a known friend of my mother and it would be in my interest to meet with her. So now I was not only excited to break my eggs, but also to meet this mysterious person from whom I was going to learn something. Not long after, she arrived and she and Tania exchanged kisses and hugs in the corridor like they hadn't seen each other for years, and yes, they indeed hadn't.

As it happened, I was introduced to Lily, who more or less knew something about me, but I had yet to find out what exactly. She was watching me most of the time while she was telling one of her hundreds of stories while she was in my father's country, and me learning that she was there made me more curious about this woman and what she possibly knew about my mother. She would have been around same age as Tania in her fifties, and they knew each other for half of that time, if not even more. Nothing had been said about my mother in their conversation, and I wasn't going to ask, at least not if I wasn't asked first about my mother. After we had finished our meal, I helped with the washing of the plates and asked to go and watch TV with Victoria in the next room, which we did. A few hours later, the two women came to the room and in a kind of pretending context, Tania excused herself and Victoria, having to help her with something in the kitchen while leaving me and Lily alone in the dining room.

Lily sat not very far from me, and I continued watching TV when she asked, "Have you met your mother?" I said yes. "How was she with you?" she asked almost immediately, like it was all of a sudden her business. I told Lily at the end what she wanted to know and even more than that. I noticed that she was highly interested in my conversation with my mother.

Then she asked me a question that I wasn't expecting in a million years: "Did your mother tell you about your sister Daniela?"

"What sister?" I caught Lily off guard almost immediately with my question. Now I could see that her face had changed all of a sudden. She was deeply concerned about something; deep down in her mind, she was worried about something that only she and my mother knew about. I was still waiting for her to answer my question, which took a while as she was trying carefully to choose her words. I could feel with my whole existence then that she was hiding something from me, and it was eating me from the inside, knowing that it could be some crucial information to my life. Her reply wasn't what I expected it to be, and of course, she took a while to choose what to say and then said she was confusing me for someone else. When she said it to me, she couldn't be any more convincing but lying. I almost believed her words and left the subject about my sister alone for later. I knew I wasn't going to get more information from Lily about Daniela. I asked her about how she met my mother and how close they were back in those days, and with me changing the subject, she was much comfortable. I pushed her even further away. My mother then met with Lily who at the time was a party person, but not only that, she was going out with the African student Armando who was from my father's country too. So Lily, my mother, and this Armando became something like an inseparable trio. My mother was in her early twenties when she'd just split up from her husband who was terrorizing her, that is, until my grandfather Rangel pulled a knife and killed my mother's husband on the spot.

My grandfather was sent to prison for attempted murder, and my mother found herself alone with her firstborn son, Angel, who was only a toddler. With the loss of her husband and father in prison, my mother then found life hard and found comfort in alcohol, and before she knew it, her son was spending more and more time with her younger sister—my aunt Zoya. The two sisters had lots of confrontation about the way my mother was leading her life, and the arguments just pushed my mother even further into the arms of her friend Armando. Both fell in love behind Lily's back, and their friendship was over then. And that was how she finished the story. It was almost impossible to imagine my mother loving a black person after all the things she said to me to my face: "black cockroach." I didn't say any of this to Lily, but there was so much of her story that puzzled me and it was about Armando. Was it possible that he was my father? I asked Lily that question, and she categorically said no. He left the country in January 1973 and I was born a year later, so he couldn't be my father. I asked if she knew who my father was. She had no idea; I almost believed her.

I suggested the name of the late president, and she replied, "It's possible. He was in Bulgaria at the time." She said that my mother was in one of the events in Hotel Rila during his visit to Pliska in June 1973. I think the excitement of having this conversation got Lily to say things she wouldn't have said under any different circumstances any other day, and she decided to end the conversation. She said she lives in Germany and she has a daughter that looks like me and would love for me to meet her one day. We shook hands goodbye as she intended to go because it was getting late, and she promised to stay in touch with me through Tania.

After she had gone, Tania and I sat for a small conversation about what was said between me and Lily; I learned a few other details from her. She mentioned that she remembers my mother being pregnant in the early seventies and she was with Armando at the time, which made Tania think that the child was his. Tania remembered that she hadn't seen my mother for a while after she gave birth away in a city called Burgas because she didn't want her family to find out that she was expecting a child from a black man. Now, this was all news for me, and the information that she gave me was begging to put the puzzle into place. I hadn't mentioned any word to Tania of "Daniela" to me from Lily, and for a fact, I knew I was born in Pliska because it was written on my birth certificate. So my mother did have a child with Armando Kanga, and she went all the way to Burgas to deliver the baby. What I needed to do now was to verify that this person "Daniela" exists and to find her if that was possible.

Back at the boarding, I had to think a lot over my conversation with Lily and especially of one thing that she said, to be more accurate, "my sister." The way Lily said my sister's name "Daniela" just like that, and she wanted to know if my mother had told me about her. This was on my mind for some time, and Lily made sure I wasn't going to ask about her again by pretending to be referring to someone else's child and being confused. I didn't believe her and knew she was hiding something, and Tania confirmed my suspicions later that day by uncovering information about my mother giving birth in Burgas without realizing how helpful this information could be for me.

Only a few months were left until the end of the school year, and I intended to do well. From school, I would go straight back to the boarding and try to avoid skinhead areas and the town center in Pavlovo, where Ivan was very likely to be there with friends and drinking beer. I would stay in my room for hours and only go down for dinner then back to the room, giving no suspicion to anyone about anything. I minded my own business and expected the same from the others, but some would tease me over the case with Ivan on my window and that I was ruining the reputation of the boarding school with the things that had happened around me. Some of the boys in the boarding school would even suggest money to sleep with me, like I was supposed to be selling myself or something. For this reason, I always stayed locked in my room. I hardly ever saw my two roommates, if ever. Sometimes when I got up early in the morning, I would find their beds untouched, like they were supposed to live in the room, but they didn't. In one of the very rare occasions when I would see them, one of them would ask me not to mention to the teachers that they don't sleep in the room, and why should I anyway? I was happy to have the room for myself.

One time, the parents of one of my roommates came to visit their daughter, only to find her not where she was supposed to be, and they turned it into a scandal for the teachers. At the end of the day, they should know where the children were in the evenings, not that anyone cared in my case where I sleep or eat when the boarding school was closed for the holidays. Anyway, the scandal led to the parents' removing their daughter from the boarding school, and shortly to follow was her friend too. Of course, nobody was there to worry about me but myself. I was told by one of the teachers in the boarding school just before the summer that since I was seventeen, I could stand a good chance to find a summer job as part-time and get paid. I liked the idea of having a job and getting paid, and at the first opportunity, I was zooming the streets in Pliska looking for the ideal places for me to work. I stopped mainly in places like retail shops because I liked clothes, plus I was studying in a school for textile and design. I was given application forms to fill out, which I would do on the spot and return with the hope of hearing from them soon. A few weeks later, a received a letter about an interview for one of the jobs I had applied for, and I was asked to be dressed appropriately. I was nervous, and it was the word *appropriately* that caused the stress. I was going to attend the interview with whatever clothes I had no matter what.

The best thing to dress myself was nice clean trousers with a clean T-shirt and a jumper if it was cold. I had only one pair of shoes and hoped that they wouldn't be looking at them necessarily if they were underneath a desk. The day came, and I was waiting among ten other girls to be interviewed for the job in one of the newly opened shops in Pliska for Dallas Jeans. Looking around, I could smell nice perfumes and see well-dressed or "appropriately dressed" girls my age. Most of them had the self-confident faces of winning the position, and some maybe knew how to do it. To be honest, it was my first ever interview and didn't know what to expect; I wasn't ready for anything. In my mind, I was thinking that all ten girls would be given jobs in the Dallas retail shop, or why else would we all be there? So in a way, I was relaxed too and waited for my turn to be interviewed, and waiting wasn't long, or should I just say, was longer than the interview. I got seated in an office with no place to hide my shoes and something like five or six people observing my behavior while writing their notes. I remember sweat going down my spine and trying to hold my breath for as long as possible before the first questions.

"Tell us something about yourself." It was so hard for me to begin with, and while I was trying to compose myself, the next question came. "Have you got any job experience in retail?" I almost wanted to lie but said no. There was silence and a few looks among them before I was asked to leave the room in a polite voice and wait outside. I waited and waited long enough to see some of the other girls that have left the room after me with delight on their faces, congratulating one another. I felt I didn't do well and yet there was hope that I might be given a chance, or why else was I sitting? Every girl had been gone when the door to the office where we were all interviewed opened and a woman came out. She sat next to me and said that she liked me and I have things to offer, which some of the other girls didn't, and she hoped I'd do better in my future interviews, wherever that might be. I left disappointed, but not discouraged.

It was the summer of 1991, and I continued looking for places to work and in the meantime stayed in Nana's apartment. She had graduated and had a month before she was leaving the country for good. Back home, she had a boyfriend with whom she had a promising future and that was all very good for her. She was also worried about what was going to happen to me when she left, and she was trying again to help by sending letters to the embassy in Moscow and the government in Africa. I had never told her about the time I went to visit Jose and his promise to help me through his brother. Nana was leaving soon, and I just didn't want to give her more worries. I was engaged in looking for a job, and one day just like that, when I was walking the streets in Pliska, I came across a bingo hall advertising for jobs that needed waitresses. I had a strong feeling that this might be it, and I wasn't wrong. I turned in to meet with the boss, who immediately was charmed by me and offered me a position to start whenever I was ready and as soon as can be.

I was ready to start almost straight away, but the problem was the uniform. The place didn't provide one, and I had to find the money to buy my skirt, black shoes, and white shirt. I knew I could ask Nana to lend me the money, but she wasn't going to be around long enough for me to pay her back. I asked Jose, but he had told me that soon there would be a delegation arriving from Moscow to pay the students, and if I'd be around long enough, I might be paid some too as the daughter of a late president. I didn't know if he was joking or being serious, but I was serious. I wouldn't let another opportunity for a job to slip through my fingers.

Another person was Ivan, and he was so pleased to see me after a few months. He was not hard to convince of how important it was for me to start this job as soon as I could, and not only did he pay for them, he drove me everywhere to find the proper waitress clothes for me to wear. I was very grateful to him for the help and let him convince me to stay in the summer house his father built somewhere in the suburban area of Pliska. I was okay for that time, working, being transported to work and back, and going to cinemas with him. I have to say he was less embarrassed to take me out on a date, but mentioning his family was always a different subject. They had learned about how he got caught with me in his bed by his ex, and his mother had threatened to leave him with nothing after she was gone if he was ever to be with me again. So he was with me again and they didn't know, or that was what I thought again before his father came one very early morning to the summer house, only to open the door to the bedroom and find us asleep. He waited long enough for Ivan to get up and tell him of his disapproval and that he wouldn't tell a word to his mother if he stopped seeing me.

Ivan, of course, didn't tell me this part and continued seeing me. We went to Student Town together a couple of times after work, and we would visit

Charlie, an architecture student from Kenya. He was selling alcohol illegally, and only those who went to his room to buy it knew of what he was doing, and Ivan was one of them.

This Charlie guy had connections with people and always offered the cheapest alcohol. He had two full fridges of beer and other alcohol like vodka, whiskey, and wine and so we were always welcomed there as long it's been paid. Ivan and I would often get eyebrows raised by other African students, some with disapproval of our relationship and especially of what had been happening at the time with all the racism in the country. They didn't like me in general going out with a white man and said I should be with black people for that matter because I wouldn't be discriminated for my color. Some of this would be so true in the future, and how little I knew of what was yet to come in my life. Anyway, it wasn't any of their business, and Ivan would get upset after a few drinks, and it would lead to a fight. If not for Charlie stopping it, only God knows how serious it could have gotten for some. Charlie was a big guy, and nobody liked to mess with him. Even after small encounters like this, we were still very welcomed to his room.

My job at the bingo hall involved taking orders from customers and serving the drinks at their tables, as well as emptying the ashtrays, which I did more often than the rest. The job paid me, but I wasn't enjoying it—going every day to work clean and smelling of good perfume and then finishing with the smell of smoked cigarettes. Ivan wouldn't care because he smoked too, but what he did care about was somebody else trying to touch me at work. The boss told me and Ivan that this was something normal, and in a place like this, I'd better get used to it if I wanted to keep the job. The problem was, I didn't want to get used to it and went to buy myself black trousers for work. That didn't go well with my boss, and he asked me to put on my skirt with which I wasn't comfortable. I challenged him, "Does it matter if I am wearing a skirt or trousers if I am doing the same job?" And yes, it did matter! In the end, I was fired. No contract signed, no money that was owed to me was paid, and I was without a job. I was disappointed and needed to find another job somewhere, and then I came up with the thought of trying the nightclub Joe in Student Town.

I knew Nicole there, and the experience with the bingo hall could help me as reference too. Unfortunately, they didn't have vacancies and I soon found myself helping them open the place at ten in the morning, setting up the tables in return for a glass of Coca-Cola. But it wasn't the drink that was bringing me to the club every morning, but pool table. The club had two pool tables, and in the mornings, I would brush the tables and then smooth them. This was the time when the club would make its money from the tables. I have seen them, many gamblers, first thing when the club doors were open. They'd run to the bar to book the tables for a few hours and start practicing shot after shot and potting the balls with an easy stroke. I found it fascinating; the cue stick held parallel with the table, and with a back-and-forth movement, the balls were potted. I would be there watching opponents arrive for the challenge, and both sides would negotiate the amount, then the rules on the black ball, and then find someone to trust to keep the money safe while they played. We, the spectators, would keep quiet at all times because of the intensity of the game when it's played for money. I would find myself a place near the table to sit and wouldn't move from it for hours. That was how I became hooked too by watching them play. Nicole would be the one to be moving often to serve other arrivals who would like to take a chance to play with the winner, and it was all for money. They all knew the rules of silence when somebody was playing and the distance that should be kept from the table. That was how I got hooked by the game, and before the club opened the doors for customers, I was practicing all the shots seeing others practice from the day before. Nicole allowed me to practice as long as I was careful with the cloth on the table. Every day became essential to me, to be there and practice before everyone else. I wouldn't know if I was doing the right stuff on the table, but what was important was potting the balls with consistency from different areas on the tables. I had a firm grip on the cue stick, and my action was steady, just like some of the guys I was watching, so much that I got carried away and even missed Nana leaving the country.

I was very sad that she didn't leave me a note of any sort. I visited Jose to find out if he had any news about me from his brother in Angola; he did have news for me, but not what I wanted to hear. He was utterly upset to see me, and I was confused with his reaction. He refused to talk to me about it, and only after I had pushed him to tell me what I had done wrong did he admit that it wasn't me. It was the secret service in my father's country that had found out about the information his brother had in his hands and the way they wanted to expose the story to the opposition media in the country. That was something that had put Jose's brother in real danger, and it wasn't known if he was still alive or not. It turned out that he was kidnapped from his house at daytime, and nobody has heard or saw anything. Now Jose had his concerns that it had something to do with my case, and he felt no longer safe. He was convinced that they, whoever they were, knew about his involvement, and it would be a matter of time before something happened to him. I just couldn't believe what I was hearing and thought that Jose was maybe rather overreacting; perhaps his brother would be back. But his face was telling it all. I got it! I should keep away from him now after what had happened to his brother and not mention it to any other countryman because according to Jose, many of them were actually government spies. Yeah right!

Anyway, I asked him if at least he could help me to be there when the embassy delegation from Moscow visited Pliska, and he promised to help me. All I needed was to ask about my sent letters to the embassy and what they were doing regarding my case. I could also send a letter through them to the government in Africa, and that way I would know that was in their hands with no excuse for not receiving it.

The day came when the delegation arrived at Pliska, and I was informed days before their arrival and was excited that maybe there might be news for me and they were just as much anticipating to meet with me, the person responsible for sending letters claiming to be the daughter of the late president of their state. Surely they would want to see me and have news for me. The room that was used for the meeting with the embassy representatives was one that was used by the students as a study room, and you could easily get twenty-plus people in there, not that it got every student in there. Many were outside, only waiting to get the money and leave. Others like me were there for personal problems waiting to be resolved, and I had Jose to count on to help me. He was going to look for an opportunity to speak alone with one of them and inform them about me and possibly arrange a time to meet face-to-face and he would translate for me. I was waiting and hoping that he did manage this. This was my moment to do something, and I was going to wait as long as it took.

It was around lunchtime in the summer of 1991, a very hot day, and if it wasn't for the embassy delegation, many of the students would be waiting in the yard like me, having a cold Zagorka beer until they passed out. This was something that the men from my father country in Bulgaria were well known for, drinking and women! It's like trying to escape from the real problems that existed in their country. Many of them were required to vote for the ruling party; of course, without the party's help, none of them would be there. So the meeting that was held in the student study room was also to inform about the current state of the country and the next year's presidential election for which the students would be expected to participate in voting for the ruling party. To me, none of this was of any interest, like who was in charge of the country and what political views the country had. I knew there was a civil war and many people had died, innocent people mostly, and here in Bulgaria, them students had a life well beyond rich people. I was wondering if the government looked that well after everyone, even the children like me left behind by Angolan servants. I was to find out all this in the future, but then and there after the meeting had finished and everyone was outside locked in a passionate conversation with others and not a word I could understand in Portuguese, I was trying to make my way to Jose.

Some of them students had an idea of why I was there, and they were the ones who thought that my being there was a complete waste of time. Maybe that was true, but I wasn't going to just walk away after the time I had waited, which was over three hours. Some of them blamed me for slowing them down, whereas they should be sitting and having a nice lunch with the representatives in a cozy restaurant of their style. Jose was there talking with one of them who had his eyes on me, nodding in acknowledgment to what he was hearing and then both walking toward me. We were introduced and shook hands as Jose was explaining things to him. He in return told Jose that never had letters of this kind been received by the embassy, and now that he had seen me, he had reason to believe that it might be true. I did remind him of another daughter, the youngest child of my father. He promised to write to the government and guaranteed that the letters would be delivered. I was pleased to hear for the first time that somebody actually didn't take my story for nonsense and would do whatever to help. Some of the students that were within hearing range might have been surprised from the conversation I had with the personnel from the embassy and more or less in the future started to take me seriously too.

It had been months since I last was in Student Town after the meeting with the representative from the embassy. I was told that would take time before I received any news and that I should be patient. I haven't been there to see Jose after that either because of his wish to keep distance with me. Ivan and I were spending more time together, and a few weeks were left before the beginning of school for me. I was still visiting Joe's club in Student Town, helping in the mornings and watching the games of pool while Ivan was working in the day. Then he would come and pick me up from the club and take me to the summer house.

We were all happy, and Ivan acted like he was so in love with me and I had no reason not to believe him. One day after he had gone to work, I was getting up to get ready to go and play pool in Student Town, when unexpectedly I felt so sick and ran to the toilet to vomit. I thought nothing at first and went on with my day as normal and at the end of the day shared with Ivan my suspicions that I might have missed my period for a month and asked if he could help me find a doctor who could examine me. We did that first thing in the morning where again I felt just as bad as the day before, and Ivan had to stop the car a few times on the way to the clinic. We got there, and I wasn't checked immediately because I had to go through registration and forms that I was asked to fill out and Ivan was frustrated to do all this because he was running late for work. At the end, like an hour later, I was reviewed by the doctor and established that my pregnancy was advanced. I was almost two and a half months' pregnant and that was the last thing I wanted then. Ivan was trying to be calm and asked the doctor if we could arrange for an abortion in the next few days, to which the doctor's response was yes but with a signed approval by a parent or guardian in this matter since I wasn't eighteen yet.

Now what? Ivan left it for me to sort this problem out since I was the one pregnant and wanted little to know about it after that. I had decided that since I was registered as living in the orphanage in Pavlovo, the director himself had to sign the papers. I had found the director's address through the help of the local police after having to explain and sign forms of some kind of security that I am who I say I am and that I live in the orphanage; just in case if he was found dead, they would have me for it. At the end, I was given his address and went by myself to his house that was located near the center of Pliska. Without too much effort, I found the place where the teacher lived. He wasn't there or he wasn't in Pliska in general, according to his wife. He was on a holiday with his children to the Black Sea, and for whatever matter I was looking for him, I wouldn't be able to reach him until the end of September, which for me was way too late for any abortion.

I explained to her the reason behind my being at her house, and all she did was sympathetically suggest that I go to the man who got me pregnant in the first place and seek to meet with his parents and perhaps they would be able to help me and that was that. She closed the door on me. I left the house determined that I need to see Ivan and discuss a variant where his parents would help sign the papers, but he wasn't having it. He wouldn't hear of such an idea, and the fact that his mother had no clue he was still seeing me would almost kill her according to him. Not just that, but he also denied having anything to do with my pregnancy, which made me so angry that I even went on to slap him across the face for calling me a "whore." He convinced himself that he wasn't the father and that I surely got pregnant in Student Town by some African student. He forbade me to call him or even go anywhere near his house, and if I tried to tell anyone in his family about it, I was going to find myself in big trouble, whatever he had in mind. It was getting very hard for me, and if Ivan had helped me before, now he wouldn't.

When the time came for me to start school, I learned that I couldn't be accepted if I was pregnant; not even part-time education was available for me. The situation wasn't any different in the orphanage either. When the director learned of my pregnancy, he said that the boarding school was for children who attended school, and since I was no longer in the school, I had to then find a place to stay. I had to beg to stay in the orphanage at least until I gave birth and after that I would resume my education, but it was refused. I had no other alternative but to pack my bag and leave the place. Tania's place was convenient for me, and I knew she would understand the circumstances

I was in, as she herself was a mother. I went there and talked with her about staying for a few nights at least until I found a permanent place to live. She was okay with that and generously let me stay for as long I wanted. I didn't just wanted to stay and do nothing, so during the day, I would go out and try to find a job and even tried the bingo hall where I worked just like months before, but I was without any success with the job hunting, some reason for being colored and too young with no experience. Tania, on another hand, couldn't help me because she herself, I learned eventually, didn't work and spent her days dating different African men.

Sometimes while she was man hunting I would be waiting in front of her apartment door for hours for her to get back and sometimes she wouldn't get back until the very early hours of the morning. I knew that her place was only temporary, and if I got a job, I would be okay to find my own place. One weekend when her daughter arrived from the boarding school, we all went to visit Lily for lunch, and this is when I met and learned that she had a daughter called Nina, named after her father Armando, the same person who fathered my mother's daughter Daniela. Lily was a very good hostess and made sure we all felt comfortable at her house. Meeting Nina and learning more about her being a daughter of Armando was a bit strange because neither Lily nor Tania had mentioned it to me in any of the conversations I had with them that Lily's daughter i Armando Kanga's. There we were, sitting at the table having lunch, and it wasn't a coincidence that I was there too. I was a child of Sonya, an old friend of Lily and Tania, who surely knew more than what they were telling me about my mother.

So Lily wanted to know if my mother knew I was pregnant. I responded with a negative shake of my head. She got up to take her plate to the sink and then said out of nowhere, "Would you like to live with me? I will be your mother." Sure, I wasn't eighteen yet at the time and according to the law I could be adopted if I wished to, but I didn't. I looked at everyone at the table including Nina to find any reaction in her eyes, but there wasn't. It's like they all knew what was coming.

Then I responded with a question: "If you adopt me, would I be able to find my father's relatives?"

She said, "No, but you can become a national of your father's country if I adopt you. I will make sure you get the name of Armando as your father." So what Lily asked me was to agree for adoption and take Armando's name as my father. Something wasn't right with the whole thing despite the fact that I was pregnant and she had offered me stability and a chance to have a family, but in exchange for what? She barely knew me and I didn't know her that well, so I gave her a hope and said I will think about it.

She offered me to stay in her apartment and spend time with Nina, like for us to get to know each other, which I liked. Nina and I had this natural relationship and understanding, like we were sisters for real. I liked spending time with her, and she introduced me to many of her friends. She was close to me, and I was close to her too in every way until she had to depart to Germany and we promised to each other to stay in touch no matter what. Lily was happy with that, and I stayed with her after Nina was gone. During the day, Lily would go to work and I would be visiting friends and before dusk I would go and meet her at the bus stop to help with the shopping she was carrying. I am not sure what, but something inside me wanted to go all the way to Burgas to find out if it was true about Daniela. I never dared to ask Lily about Daniela, and I had to get the answers from someplace else. So one day I told Lily that I would be away for a few days to visit the orphanage in Preslavo that I missed so much since I moved to the city. She, of course, didn't mind at all and, above all, gave me money. I hated what I was doing, but I needed to do it and it wasn't just for myself, but for my sister Daniela too.

I got on the train to Burgas and was there after a six-hour-long journey. I went straight to the register's office where I waited for like half an hour because I was very early. I was the only person to be waiting at that time and couldn't help but notice that everyone who walked nearby looked at their watch and then at me. I got in soon after the office opened its door and told the woman sitting behind a small window, which she had to open to hear me well. I was looking for my sister's birth certificate and acted as though I knew what I was doing. She got up and asked which year was my sister born, and now I got stuck. I didn't know what year she was supposed to be born, but I wasn't going to show any signs of uncertainty and came up with seventy-one. She asked next for her name, and I quickly answered back the name of my sister with Armando at the end. She started cruising through the pages as she was trying to get over with me and returned to her desk, hoping for the next person to be someone who knew what he or she was doing.

She couldn't find anything in the registering book for 1971 and was almost certain now that I was not sure of what I was looking for and was wasting her time. She put the book in its place and asked me to come back when I had some information about the person concerned. I felt that I couldn't just leave like that empty-handed, coming all the way from Pliska, no way. I knew I could win her sympathy if I just told her the truth about myself. I explained that my mother gave birth to a girl in Burgas in the early seventies and that I needed to establish a connection with my sister. It looked that this worked because the office lady asked me next for my mother's name, which I was comfortable to provide. She looked from the book of seventy-two and three since I was born seventy-four, and since my sister was older than me, it has to be in one of the two books. I was asked to sit in the corridor and wait. Now I waited with other people who have come after me and who maybe had more important reasons to be there than me. So I waited and was hoping that the woman would come out soon with some good news.

She came out with a smile on her face like for her it mattered too. She was carrying the birth certificate of my sister Daniela, which she happily handed to me. She explained how hard it was to find it because my mother had my sister's names changed. First she was named after my mother's main and surname and a year later she has been recognized by her father Armando. After all that, I really had a sister Daniela, and she was born 1972, two years older than me, a sister! My journey back to Pliska was more pleasant with the proof I had in my hands, a proof which Lily couldn't deny. She was hiding something, that is for sure, and if she had a daughter with Armando and my mother had a daughter with the same man, how could you not mention something like that unless you were hiding something? I was determined more than ever to find out about the deep secret that Radi was hiding from me and how I was connected to that secret. Another thought never left my mind: if my mother had a daughter with a black man and she didn't want anything to do with black people, why did she get involved again and had me?

It was going to be almost impossible to find the truth from Lily by asking her, so what I did was show her the birth certificate of my sister, which she stared at for a while and then she went pale. "You had no right to do that!" Lily said.

"Of course I have, she is my sister!" I defended myself. Lily then unexpectedly grabbed me by my throat with all the power she had in her hand, and I screamed out of pain, trying to release from her hold. She saw me struggling to breathe and then said, "I will kill you if you dare say something to anyone" and then she let me free.

I got my stuff out of her house and now I was scared because I didn't know what I had done to trigger her actions. She was scared of something and it was to do with me, whatever that was. I knew that this would break my relationship with Nina, her daughter in Germany, and she would tell her whatever she wanted and Nina would believe her. I was devastated about that because I really liked Nina and she liked me. I went to Tania and stayed there the night, only to be told in the morning that I couldn't go to her house anymore and that she was scared of what Lily might do to her. So it was obvious that Lily had phoned Tania and asked her to get rid of me and Tania would just obey her. These women were not so nice to me all of a sudden; I was a threat to them and especially Lily. I was pregnant and had no place to go. I tried to see Ivan a few times after I went to his house, and his mother opened the door and then shouted to Ivan who was in the middle of having lunch that the "Negro woman is here to see you!" He wouldn't even make an effort to come to the door to see me, yet he knew that I needed him to help me. His mother's insult was nothing to me as I already got it from my own mother once and her own son and those were people that I loved and hurt me the most.

I couldn't remember how many nights I slept at the train station after that, but they were too many. I used to smell a lot, my clothes were disgustingly old, especially for a job interview I didn't dare try. I picked leftovers from tables, and that wasn't enough. I was really skinny and had lost lots of weight—a complete mess. Winter was approaching and I needed a shelter, and the only nice person I could think of was Charlie from Kenya in Student Town. He saw the state I was in, and as there were people in his room drinking beer, he asked them to leave as he used some excuse and gave me some clean clothes and let me shower and eat. He was with his girlfriend in the room and had a spare bed on which I slept for months.

Whenever Charlie went to lectures, me and his girlfriend Petia would sleep till late and would get up at lunchtime. Charlie would get back from university around two in the afternoon with some video movies and always a Coca-Cola for me. He didn't have to do this for me, but he did it. I was his younger sister and he was there to protect me, and I think I liked being protected. Days turned into months, and I was months away from giving birth to a baby. Charlie and Petia were excited for me and were coming up with names for the baby, and around that time, Ivan showed up many months after to see if I was okay. Words can't describe how happy I was to see him; after all, he was the father of my baby and I needed him regardless.

Charlie refused to let him in the room, and I had to go out to speak with him. He was saying how much he missed me, and it wasn't because of that I let him near me but his desire to help me get a place through the social services, a place to live with the baby and him. Charlie understood the importance of this and was sad to see me move away. We promised to stay in touch and he would visit me after I had given birth to the baby. I moved to an apartment given to me by the social services, which consisted of a single room with a small entrance and a common bathroom on each floor. The room I was given had nothing else but a single bed. Ivan volunteered to bring me a fridge, a small stove for cooking, of which he did neither.

It was Charlie who called the dorm one day and asked to speak with me. He came to visit me later in the week with a friend who was driving a small van to carry a small secondhand TV, stove, and fridge. All this Charlie did for me and for nothing in return. So pretty much I was comfortable, having my own place for which I had to pay rent that wasn't much, but considerably a lot for someone who hasn't got a job like me. I had the time in the world to think if I wanted to keep the baby or leave it for raising for three years and then have him or her back, but never for adoption like my mother did for me and my sister Daniela. I wanted to continue with my study and at the same time I didn't want to leave my child in the care of the government.

In my mind, I believed that once I got in touch with my father's family, the life for me and my child would be much better and away from racism. I believed that things could change for me one day. Ivan promised to help me with whatever he could, but wouldn't recognize the child as his own. He still believed that I had slept with someone else and he was only helping me because he had some small feeling for me. I would spend the next few months waiting to give birth and all I was doing was reading books and watching TV. The dorm where I stayed was full of single mothers or families who were so poor and had no other place to stay. Some people looked wealthy enough not to be living in the dorm, but that was decided by others. I was happy to have a roof above my head and wasn't much of a person to go out and especially since I didn't have much money. I always stayed distanced from people; I know many meant no harm, but just in case, I never let myself trust anyone and avoided borrowing money even when I didn't have any. One of my neighbors had a baby boy who was like a month old, and she was single. Often she would be screaming at her baby for no reason and put all this down to the problems she had with the father of the child. He was an alcoholic and wasn't committing himself to her and the child. Having seen that, I knew I couldn't be forcing Ivan into marriage just because we had a child, but I would have expected him to recognize it as his when the time came.

I was expected to give birth on the ninth of March 1992 and had no concerns regarding the pregnancy. I had been many times to visit my gynecologist, and he assured me that the baby was developing well and I should have nothing to worry about. Ivan was checking on me regularly like after he finished work, he would come to see me for a little while and then he would go home. I suppose he was doing it to avoid the scenario where I would go and look for him at his house and his parents would find out.

The time when I least expected it, I was reading my book in bed one night when a sharp pain in my stomach made me panic. It must have been in the very early hours of the morning on the twentieth of February when I realized that something was happening and I had nobody to call for help. My instinct was telling me to go to Ivan and wait for him when he is leaving early for work. I did just that. I managed to get to the bus stop and wait there for an hour or even more. I got on the bus that took me near to where

Ivan lived and waited in the garden. As I was expecting, he was the first to get up for work and he could help me by taking me to the hospital and be there for me. He was surprised to see me there so early in the morning, and I explained that I was experiencing some pain in my stomach and if he could help me get to the hospital. He looked at me like I was some stranger to him and said he was running late for work because of me. He told me to go to the hospital by myself and later he will check on me when he finishes work. I followed what he said and went back home to get changed because my water had broken and my trousers were really wet. All this was new to me, and I was scared of what might happen. I needed someone to be next to me when I was going through all this, and funny enough, I wanted my mother to be the one.

Anyway, I got to the clinic in the end with lots of stopping and holding on the sidewalks with spasms. Many people were waiting inside for different issues, and I was waiting in line when I shouted out of pain and was holding my stomach. Everyone looked at me with shock, coming to terms that I was about to deliver. Time was not something I had, and before I knew it, I was in an ambulance driving with the siren on through the streets of Nina. I was admitted, changed into a dress, and asked if I had next of kin to be contacted. Asked if I had relatives that I wished them to contact, I gave Ivan's name and place of work. Then I was put into a bed next to a woman that had been in labor for over ten hours and in massive pain. She was asking for painkillers, and the nurse was refusing to give them to her as the screams continued. As for myself on the other hand (I must have experienced the same pain as the woman next to me), I was trying to stop the screams. I could feel I was somewhere very close to giving birth, and when the nurse came to check on me, she confirmed my suspicions and rushed me to the delivery room, where bodies of nurses were getting ready for me.

I was scared and shaking, looking to capture some familiar face around me, but there was nothing. I was positioned comfortably and ready to follow the instructions of the nurse. I did as many pushes as I could until I heard that sweet sound of a baby cry! It filled me up with joy and happiness that was so hard for me to describe. I looked up to see the baby, and there she was hanging upside down while the nurse held her legs. She was so beautiful and innocent, and I knew she would never experience the same fate I had.

She was taken away almost immediately after that, and I was put in a bed with wheels in the hallway while they found a room with a spare bed for me. I must have been asleep soon after they moved me to the corridor because I remember the nurse who came to wake me up from a very deep sleep, needing me to move to another bed. She helped me walk to the room and put me into the bed that I found ever so comfortable, and before she walked away, I asked her if I could see my baby and if she was okay. The nurse smiled and said the baby girl would be with me in a few days' time because she was so small and she wouldn't be able to survive on my milk only. She was placed in an incubator for support, and she was fine. It was obvious she was born under the standard weight which was partly my fault, but all I wanted then was to hold her in my arms.

I was devastated a few hours later when four nurses each brought a baby wrapped in a soft cloth and gave them to the women in my room and I was the only one without, staring at the rest of them. I could see the way they were breastfeeding and how relaxed both mother and baby were. The time the mothers and babies spent was four or five times a day for an hour's session, long enough to connect. On the day when I was given my daughter for the first time, I was so emotional and cried with joy to hold her next to me. She was so small and could barely open her eyes. She was so gently wrapped in soft white cotton, and the only part of her body I could see was her head, which was enough for me at that point. I was able to recognize some features of her father on her face, like the shape of the mouth and the small dimple in the chin, something her father had. I was looking at her even when breastfeeding her, completely hypnotized by her, and I could tell she enjoyed being held by me. When the time came to be parted, she was unsettled from my arms by the nurse and started crying. My heart "sank a ball" and sealed the moment in which I decided never to leave her. So that was the first encounter with my daughter and the only one for that day, as exhaustion engulfed me and I missed the next time for feeding due to sleep.

It was Saturday evening very late on the twenty-second of 1992, when a man was shouting outside the windows and sounded more like he was drunk. I could vaguely hear what he was screaming only after one of the women in my room decided to open the window wide open to shout back at the intruder, which I thought was totally inappropriate for her to do. It was a cold February night, and we were all wearing pajamas. Was it coincidence that she opened the window to a man who was looking for me? Believe it or not, he was asking for me, to see me while he was drunk standing outside and waking the whole building. I had no other choice but to show my face through the window and tell Ivan to come tomorrow if he wanted to see his child, and I shut the window behind me. He was there for a little while singing of excitement for his child. The following day, he showed up, and I would be lying if I said it didn't matter to me. He was there to make amends and to see his daughter with his own eyes. Even though he was unable to touch her, it was good to see her through the window that separated us. For health and safety for the babies, families were not allowed to have physical touch, which was to do with some virus going around at the time. Ivan was drunk again and without the restriction on that day, I would have not let him touch my daughter anyway.

He recognized the fact that she looked like him and he would like to be part of her life, something I never had forbidden him. We didn't talk about how I managed to get to the clinic on the day I was in labor, or if he got in trouble for being late that morning, or even where he was for the last couple of days since I gave birth to our child. Nothing! I asked him if he would like to come on Monday to give his name and recognize his daughter, and he was positive that he wouldn't miss it for anything. I was happy not much for me but for the baby that her father had agreed to recognize her on paper; after seeing her, he had no doubt that she was his.

It wasn't, of course, as expected. First thing on Monday morning, the hospital administrator came to see me so that we could have my daughter's name registered and receive a birth certificate. Yet I was waiting for Ivan to arrive any time and asked if we might wait until the father of my child comes after work and this should be before 3:00 p.m. She didn't mind at all, and she didn't mind even after 4:00 p.m. and the following day too. But he wasn't coming, and I had to admit to myself I was better off without him.

I gave my daughter my name and named her Luiza, one of the characters from the latest book I was reading at the time. Her father was nowhere to be seen for months. I didn't even bother looking for him; if he wanted to come and be with us, he knew where we lived. We spent a whole long month in the hospital waiting for my sweet little angel to put on some kilograms in order to be released from special care. I needed to be there next to her. Some of the nurses were very caring toward me and supplied me with some old baby clothes, knowing that I couldn't afford to buy them. Some even suggested I should consider leaving my daughter for three years in government care and to enable me to work or continue to study, but the problem with that was I wasn't going to be allowed to have access to her during the three years. It was good to have advice from people with more life experience than me, but the experience I had wasn't really the same as what they had.

It was all a new life for me and my daughter, living in a small room with nobody to disturb us. I was having a woman from the social services coming once a week to see if we needed anything. A place to eat was for free for me, and all done by the services. I would be given coupons, which I'd take to a local school canteen, and they without any questions asked served me food. With my daughter, it was a different matter when it came to food. Her food I had to buy with the allowances I would receive every month, and it was mainly puree made of a variety of vegetables and fruits.

Charlie had come to visit us on many occasions and bought a pram for my daughter, which made a significant contribution toward going more outside during the day as opposed to sitting on the balcony. I had no words of gratitude enough to express my thanks for the things he had done for me and my daughter. He also bought a swing bed for her, which Luiza so loved sleeping on. My daughter was a year old when I found her a friend, a boy of similar age living across the corridor with his single mother, who was a part-time nurse called Daniela.

She would trust me with her son whenever she needed to run to the shop and get supplies and sometimes I would do the same. We trusted each other because there was nobody else. One of those days when she was out and about, I had both children in my apartment playing while I was watching TV. None of them could talk yet, and all they made was noises sounding similar to something but nothing, really. That moment, my daughter was holding a toy that belonged to Miro, and as she was trying to give it to him, she rose to her feet and started walking toward him. She was realizing what was happening because her whole face was lit up in a smile and excitement through her movements. I was about to jump to my feet, all panicked that she might fall and hurt herself on a desk when I realized that this was the moment I should remember forever and let her walk and she was doing so well. Smiling, she reached the nearest table and held herself on to it and then walked back to where she was sitting and did it as many times as she could; my eyes were filled with tears of joy at what I was witnessing. I opened my arms to her and she ran to me, losing her balance at the end, but I was there to hold her.

Time went by, and we did well just the two of us, with help from friends and the social. I knew Ivan wasn't going to recognize his daughter voluntarily, and I sought advice from the social workers on how to have him pay child support, knowing little that making this choice was going to devastate me forever. I went one day to visit Ivan at his workplace, knowing when he finished work. He wasn't very pleased to see me, of course; he had moved on with his life and so had we. He might have suspected that I was coming not just to say hello but there was more to it, like his daughter, for example, that he hadn't seen for years. I was straight with him and explained how important it would be for my daughter to have a father in her life and also if anything happened to me she would be left in the orphanages, and that was something I couldn't let happen.

He understood that I meant serious conversation and something he needed to consider seriously as I was trying to have him do it voluntarily, yet if he refused, I would take legal action against him. He acted as if he was going to do it anyway but needed to speak with his family first about it. I gave him an "okay, I understand" attitude. I made him understand that my daughter came before everything and everyone else, and time was also important for me as she was two years old and ready to start kindergarten and that required monthly payments. I was, on the other hand, going to look for a job and try to get back to finish the two remaining years of my school as a part-time student. He promised to get back to me soon after he had spoken with his family and particularly his mother because she was the one that made the decisions in the house.

Weeks turned into months and I had yet to hear from him when I finally decided that it was enough and showed up at his parents' house long enough to meet with his mother and tell her that I have a child with her son. Ivan wasn't there, and that made things easier as she was a woman and despite the fact she didn't like me for being black, she knew how it felt to be a single mom. It all did come as a shock to her, having to learn that her son had been seeing me after she had forbidden him. She wanted to see the child for herself before she made any conclusions as to her son being the father, and we arranged for the next day. She arrived at the apartment to see Luiza, and she acknowledged her as a granddaughter. She then made the decision that her family was obligated to help for Luiza's well-being and that Ivan would have to recognize the child. Ivan did recognize her weeks later on May 27, 1994, in my presence, and now that he had done that, it was his right as her father to spend time with her. I had never forbidden him to visit her whenever he wished to or even take her to his house for the weekend where his parents also enjoyed her company. That gave me time off too, and I was able to look for jobs in the meantime and also push the matter with my family forward through the embassy by sending letters almost every week and waiting for replies.

It wasn't long before I learned that a delegation was arriving in Bulgaria from Moscow that same year in the summer, and a man called Lima would like to meet with me as he had some news for me from the African government. I was ready and excited to meet Mr. Lima that day when he invited over twenty countrymen students for lunch at a nice restaurant in Student Town. I was there on the same table sitting next to him, and Masuka, the president of the students, was translating to me once again. I was told then that the government was aware of me and they did believe that I was the daughter of the late African president. I was asked by Mr. Lima to bring in person the following day a copy of my birth certificate and two pictures for my new national passport. He promised that my life would change and I should be able to study anything I wanted in the future. So with that promise, I left Student Town and focused on my daughter, believing for a better life one day for both of us.

I informed Ivan of the situation and a possibility for me and my daughter traveling to Africa to meet with my father's family and that I was only waiting for my new national passport. The news wasn't something he wanted to hear as he was getting to know his daughter, and that was what turned everything around for me. Without discussing anything with me, his parents influenced him to take custody of the child, something to that point never occurred to me he would do. He did it! On July 1995, Ivan won custody over our daughter on the basis that his family had a lot more to offer to the child and that I was a single parent with no family and only had support from the government. For that matter, Ivan also used pictures taken of the single room I lived with my daughter, who was growing and needed a better environment. They had a house with a garden and money to provide her with a good education when she was ready, and Ivan also used my relationship with Africans suggesting it wasn't good for his daughter to be culturally confused with her ethnicity. They had a lawyer representing what would be in the child's interest. I had nobody in my corner to defend me. I was heartbroken that day, and standing in the courtroom, I just wished the ground would open and swallow me.

I was told that I could have my daughter every two weeks for the weekend, and that was supposed to make me feel better? I had to call Ivan to arrange when and how we meet for me to have my daughter; that was so painful. Holding her after two weeks of not seeing her didn't make me feel good but worse. At that moment, I hated living, I hated myself, my mother, my father's family, everyone who didn't do anything for me when I needed them, and I hated myself for being who I was. I needed to stop the pain and made it easier when I stopped going to see my daughter for a while. I was praying that something happened soon for me and I'd be recognized as my father's daughter and could then win my daughter back. There was no news from Africa, and the letters I had sent over and over were unanswered.

I wasn't going to end up like some of the girls from the orphanages—prostitutes, beggars, or thieves. I had to find a way but didn't know how, and the only way that naturally came to me was by playing pool. I got obsessed playing pool in the mornings and spent hours and hours watching good players, which helped me avoid thinking of my daughter, whom I missed so badly. I never had money, but it all started when somebody as a joke decided to bet on me and split the half and, next thing I knew, I got hooked on it.

I won game after game and made money for me and for others. To me, the money I was winning was significant enough to have food on my table and to buy presents for my daughter, and still, none of this would heal the pain I felt in losing my daughter. What things will they be telling her about me, how will she act when I next see her? Thoughts like that had pushed me away from the one thing I love the most in my life. I got involved in tournaments of pool and took it seriously as a sport. I moved out of the social services building and found a place on my own and joined a full-time job in the day as a general worker in construction business, where I had to do what a man does, from mixing cement and transferring it by pushing it on a cart; that was every day from nine to five. I got good money to live well, and yet playing pool for money was something that thrilled me. I found finally that I was good at something, and that made me feel good about myself. I didn't have many friends and sometimes would go out after work with my colleagues for a beer and then home to my flat that I was renting to sleep. The weekends would be off work, and that was when I would enter pool competitions where I would be the only girl among thirty boys and men, but that wouldn't bother me a single bit. I have lost so much already to that point to care what anybody thought of me, I would just focus on my game and the rest is history! If I lost my games early, I would go to see Charlie from Kenya and spend hours in his room alongside many who just sat there drinking and chatting away in different African dialects. I even tried to pay Charlie back the money he lent me, but he wouldn't have it. I would just sit there and watch a movie that Charlie had rented from the video shop and focus on the movie although I wouldn't be able to understand it because it was in the English language. One of these late evenings I met Victor, a man from Zuland. He was a third-year electrical engineer student in the Technical University of Pliska. He offered to escort me to the bus stop one very late night, as he was worried for my security or that was just the pretext to declare his love for me. He had apparently spotted me in Charlie's room, and for weeks was looking for an opportunity to talk with me.

I wasn't much into dating anyone at the time, especially with the way I was treated by Ivan, but Victor had this innocence about him and I thought why not. He deserved a chance and so did I. So we started seeing each other, like twice a week, and he was very patient with me about taking the relationship to the next level. I didn't know if that wasn't also down to Charlie who had brotherly protection over me. Victor had a few years left to graduation and was serious about taking me away to Zuland with him, but knowing that I couldn't just leave my daughter behind made it even harder.

In the meantime, I had dedicated myself to finding my sister Daniela at whatever cost. So I went to the hospital where she was born in Burgas and presented myself as her sister. Obviously, many years had passed since she was there and not many hospitals kept records of release for children left for adoption—that is, if she was given for adoption. I learned that she was taken home by my mother in Pliska and that shocked me at first because none of this made any sense to me. Why did she give me up for adoption and not my sister before me? Where is she now? What happened to her? My mother never mentioned to me the existence of my sister Daniela; she was obviously hiding something, and she would be the last person to tell me the truth. So I improvised and went to the local city hall of her residency and asked to pull up a copy of her birth certificate, and to make things easier this time, I brought with me my birth certificate with her name on it. They gave me a copy for a small payment, which I was able to provide, and from the details on her birth certificate, I was able to see her place of birth and the names of her parents or my grandparents.

The next thing, I was on a bus to the village of Tran, a place located near the border with Serbia and where more or less four thousand people lived in it. I got there and again used the local registrar to establish any relatives of mine in the village, and I did find a relative who was supposed to be a husband of my grandfather's sister and who remembered my mother yet had never heard of me. He was helpful though to give me enough information of the area where my grandmother lived in Pliska, and with this, I was on the way back to the capital.

So I was doing everything behind my mother's back. She had no idea what I was up to, and I only hopped she wouldn't find out before I found my grandmother, her mother. Lucky for me that I didn't have to go through the registrar to find my grandmother as she was there in the phone book. I found the phone number and used it to get the address through the public inquiry phone. I got all the courage in me to face her with the suspicion and fear that she must have heard from my mother that I had showed up at her house and she had given me the stick.

However, I had nothing to lose and was ready to knock on her door when the elevator door behind me opened and a man stepped out and walked toward me. He was surprised to find me there just as much as I was surprised that somebody would be visiting my grandmother before lunch. He asked who I was and what I was doing at his grandmother's. Now that was something I didn't expect, really! This man was my brother Angel, and he had no clue that I was his sister.

My instinct told me to leave and not say anything, but I was there and would never get a second chance to speak with him again. I didn't know him, and he could have called the police if he wished to. I revealed myself to him and the reasons I was there, hoping that he would believe me and though not necessarily wish to help me. To my surprise, he was not shocked by what I told him and, after he had seen my birth certificate, he accepted that I was his sister. The next thing, we both got inside the apartment and my grandmother, bless her, needed no introduction as to who I was. She offered me a cup of tea, and my brother Angel sat next to me listening to my story that I was telling my grandmother as tears welled in her eyes. She had given up on my mother years ago when her husband, my grandfather, died. My mother was always on her own, not caring about her or my aunt, and now she wanted to make some amends for that. My grandmother felt that my mother should have done better for me and my sister; she wanted me to move in with her and look after me, but it was too late.

My brother rang my mother from the other room while we were talking, and in a short span of time, she arrived at the door shouting at him and then me. My grandmother asked her to calm and sit down, which she did; we all had to have a civilized conversation. My mother asked why they let me in and threatened if I didn't leave she would call the police, and of course, those were just words of a woman that was put in a room with people who wanted different answers for themselves. The one I needed was "my sister" and where she was and I promised to leave her alone after that. She exploded when she heard my sister's name and became uncontrollable! My brother had to calm her down, and only then did she reveal that my sister had been left in an orphanage in Pliska and she wasn't given for adoption, which made me believe that she knew what had happened to her. My mother wouldn't give me any more information on my sister, and just to top it off at the end, as I was leaving, she said, "If you want to play Sherlock Holmes, you should know your brother is in an orphanage too." I pretended that I didn't hear then left the apartment followed by Angel, who wanted to be by my side and really meant it.

That was the only time I met with my grandmother before she died. We went to Angel's workplace where I was introduced as his sister to his colleagues and then we went to his wife's workplace and had a cup of coffee. We spent the rest of the day together, and he told me that he knew of the existence of his sisters that were mixed race and left in orphanages. He also remembered a detailed fight between my mother and her sister involving one of the daughters and that her father was sending the money for her and she didn't get any because she was in an orphanage. I promised Angel to stay in touch with him. I focused my thoughts on finding my sister; I had the feeling that probably, like me, she was lost in this country and needed somebody to love her. I was going to be strong for both of us and would make sure we would never be apart once I found her. I traced her last address in an orphanage in Pliska and learned that she had died when she was only five years old.

With tears, I left the building with my heart broken. Not her! This can't be true. She must be still alive. I could feel with my whole existence that something wasn't right in this whole situation. Why didn't my mother tell me that she had died? Surely she would know and spare me the pain of finding it out. She can't be that cruel, can she? She would have even buried the body because my sister wasn't given for adoption. Something wasn't right, and this is when that inner voice made me turn and walk back toward the orphanage. I had questions to ask about her death and needed to see the death certificate of my sister to really believe her dead. I spoke with two different women who had worked there since that time. This is where my suspicions were confirmed that someone was lying. One said she died of pneumonia, and the other claimed she was found with a wound on her head caused by falling on the toilet plate. Now I had my reasons to push to find more of what really happened to her, and my next place of visit was the registrar where her death certificate would be. Boom! She had no death certificate, and in the hospital where she would have been accepted after her death for an autopsy, there were no records of that year for the same person. Now that was serious and needed serious investigation, so I informed the local authorities and the police.

In the meantime, I was still waiting for some news from the embassy in Moscow. One evening in the summer of 1996, I met an old acquaintance from my childhood years in the orphanage in Preslavo on the way to some TV talk show where he was taking part of, and he didn't mind me coming along. I never got the chance to ask what it was about because we were too busy chatting away about the past and current, and the next thing I found myself was in the backroom of the national TV among makeup artists ready to do my face. I surely shouldn't be there and was about to walk out when the journalist that was leading the show stopped me and said that my contribution would mean a great deal to many children like me.

So I changed my mind and stayed during the show, and even if I wanted to leave, it would have been impossible because I was seated on the very front row next to the projectors, which was pointed in my face each time the camera was focused on us. There were like five or six of us sitting and waiting to be interviewed of our life's experiences in the orphanages and how we coped with life on our own. I wasn't ready for this, and certainly the last thing I wanted was for people's sympathy on the other side of the camera.

When the microphone was put into my face and I was asked, "Tell us something about yourself," I was confused and the few seconds I took to answer felt like hours with all eyes on me. The moment had arrived when I was supposed to introduce myself to a million viewers. The next question gave me the push to do it: "What was life for you being colored? How does it affect you?" Well, I went on and expressed myself without holding anything, and the journalist was enjoying it. She found my story intriguing and not only her, but the million viewers also, who, after the show, wouldn't stop ringing and asking to meet with me, even women ready to adopt me! One woman claimed she knew me from the age of two; now that was a person I wanted to meet to surely learn something about my past.

Stefka was very happy to meet with me days later in her flat, where her two daughters who were of the same age as me were sitting at the table, as their mother was opening a very old picture album. I knew she had something about my past, and I was about to find out what it was. She has been working in the kindergarten for twenty years, and she said that her late sister's dream was to adopt me and she never could. Now this was something that gave me such a surprise because I didn't remember any of this. She explained that her sister lost her daughter as a baby and she was devastated. Soon after that, she visited the place where Stefka worked and fell in love with a colored girl that would always hide in the trees and was hardly noticeable. She did everything she could to adopt me and even took the case to court because although I was given up for full adoption and signed by my mother, someone was trying to stop the process of adoption. Then weeks later, an attempt was made to kidnap me by two men from my father's country and I was only three years old. The police were patrolling the kindergarten for weeks, and her sister never got the chance to adopt me and that devastated her even more.

All this happened in 1977 and spooky! Around the same period of my sister's supposed death. I had to put the puzzle together, and it wasn't hard to eventually do it. Now that I had found and proved Daniela's existence, it was a matter of time before the police were to find anything on her. I told Nina in a letter about Daniela. She needed to know about her, especially if the two shared the same father. She went to ask Lily, her mother, about it, who swore to kill me and my daughter if she saw me. I guess Nina never knew of Daniela's existence, and that made things interesting. Why would Lily not tell Nina about Daniela? And yet really, she didn't mean to tell me either; only my persuasion forced it.

Months later, Nina arrived in Bulgaria, and we secretly met to talk about Daniela. Nina was just as scared of her mother finding about me and her and knew only one place where her mother wouldn't go—her own mother's place, Nina's grandmother. We were there having lunch one afternoon when her grandmother joined us at the table, and she, without realizing it, put the puzzle together for me. I was sitting in front of Daniela herself, having lunch. How is that possible? Lily, in a story that her mother was telling us, couldn't have children as she was barren. That was it! I couldn't tell anything to Nina about my suspicions then and about the possibility that she is Daniela. I asked her later when alone in which hospital she was born, but she didn't know. We promised to stay in touch despite Lily's opinion. I was sure I was on the right track, and I was going to confront my mother with it.

I went to her despite everything and confronted her. She admitted to having used my sister Daniela as bait. Armando helped by informing my father about my existence when he arrived as a president officially to Bulgaria in 1976 to meet with the president of Bulgaria. He was informed at a dinner that many senior students from his country were invited also. He was going to arrange to have me back to Africa without knowing that my mother had given me for adoption. When Stefka's sister wanted to adopt me, it became a critical moment for my mother and she had to find a lawyer to help her have me back, and this was why Stefka's sister faced the challenge of adopting me. Time was running out for her because nothing was as simple as my mother thought it would be, and she needed to go through a long legal process to have me back and time wasn't what she had.

My father wanted me, and this was when she got involved with the African (countrymen) students to try to kidnap me, only for them to fail. The only option left for her was to get my sister Daniela and pay whoever to have the trace of her disappearance covered. Daniela was used as me, and not long before that, my father would know that she wasn't his daughter and the truth was revealed to him. Armando was sent to prison back in his country in 1977 later that year for conspiracy, and my mother stopped receiving money for "my support." The question was what will happen to Daniela, and that wasn't very far to think of because my mother's friend Lily couldn't have children and she loved Armando once, so she took Daniela and raised her as her own daughter. She created a new birth certificate for her and gave her a proper home, as opposed to her going back to the orphanage. All this just because my father was a president and my mother needed the money. I could have had the chance to be adopted and have a family, and because of all this, I was the one paying the price. I couldn't tell the police that my mother was involved in conspiracy against the former African president and that my sister was kidnapped by some crazy psycho. I didn't want to take away from her the only mother she has ever known to have. Knowing all that happened didn't make me feel any better because my mother had her life she made for herself, thanks to the money my father was sending to her "for me" and yet she wasn't willing to help me with my father's family.

I carried on with my life on the construction site and with saving money, as I had made the decision to travel to Moscow and visit the embassy. I was going to try to travel to Africa from there, and I was hoping to be given a visa. At work, everyone learned about my past through the TV show and later the newspaper, as I had a friend writing the full story in a weekly edition. Charlie wanted to see the article, which only happened to be published the following day after he traveled back home to Kenya for good. I felt like I had lost my brother. Of course, the story in the newspaper wasn't seen as appropriate by some figures in my father's country, who learned about it through the students in Bulgaria. Weeks later, in one of my visits to Student

Town, I was stopped by a few countrymen and one of them slapped me across my face and called me a "whore" and a "liar" and I was threatened to be killed if I didn't withdraw my story and deny what I have said before. That was something I was never going to do; furthermore, I was motivated to go to Moscow and speak face-to-face with the people who wanted me to keep quiet on that matter. Before, if I only had skinheads against me, now I had them and Lily.

In the meantime, I was avoiding Student Town and contacts with the African students or those who were close to them. Lily, on the other hand, was visiting the place every other day because she was dating a man half her age from my father's country. She learned that I knew everything, and that made her even more dangerous to me. On January 17, 1997, I traveled to Moscow and stayed in a hotel for a whole week near Sheremetyevo, quite near from the embassy by choice. I managed to meet with Mr. Viegas, who was the consular at the time, and he arranged for me a meeting with the ambassador, the same ambassador whom I met in Bulgaria years back. I was on my own with the ambassador, and I requested to be given a visa so that I could travel and meet with my father's family in Africa. The ambassador suggested that it wouldn't be a good idea for me to go there without having a place to stay and initiated to phone one of the sisters of my late father. While we were at his office, he had the contact numbers ready by his side and dialed them. On the other side of the line, somebody must have answered because he went on talking in Portuguese, sort of explaining something. It lasted no more than five minutes, and then he turned toward me and said that he spoke with one of the sisters of my father, not mentioning which one exactly, and she won't accept me in Africa.

He then said I should go back to Bulgaria and that he was going to send a fax to whoever was concerned with my case and I should wait for news. I was disappointed to have gone all the way for nothing and having to spend money for it. I was just being played around with promises by Mr. Lima back three years ago and no word since, and now the embassy was telling me to wait a little bit more. I was really getting sick with the whole thing and focused my mind on my pool, where on a weekly basis I was playing in tournaments and not winning anything. Overall, I didn't have anyone to coach me, and my strategic game was very weak. I did reach the very first tournament finals for women in 8 ball and lost it against Maria, a friend of mine. She was dating many pool players, whether was on purpose to help develop her game, I don't know, but I have to say it did help her. However, it was her ex who was the referee on the final match and more or less played his part well. I did well to be in the finals of the first women's pool competition, where over sixty participants took part and won some cash for second place.

After that, not many women took part in the following tournaments and they were dropped, so players like me and Maria were the only ones left to compete against the men.

My life continued in that direction for a year, where I would visit my daughter who was five years old and would take her for a day out either at the cinema or the zoo and then bring her back home to her father. On another day, I would go out with Victor who was always patient with me as he always came second when it came to my daughter and pool. He would take me out for a nice dinner and then the cinema, and if I wished, I stayed with him the night. I couldn't really see my future with him because everything for me was in Bulgaria, my daughter, my pool competitions, and I had to wait for news from Angola. On the other hand, he was promising me so much that nobody else would do for me, like a better life with a chance to continue with education in Zuland and become whoever I wanted, and he was going to help me do that once he got a job as an engineer in a company that was run by his uncle. The thing was, I wasn't sure of anything at that point, but I wanted to be happy and to have somebody loving me for who I was and Victor did just that. With him, I was normal and safe. When the moment arrived after he graduated as an engineer from the Technical University of Pliska on July 13, 1997, he had only months before leaving for good back to Zuland, his home. Then for the first time in my life, I saw all the disappointments I was going to leave behind and the positive move somewhere with a fresh start in a country where I wasn't going to be seen as black.

Victor traveled home in September and left me his address and phone in Zuland. He promised to call me every week at a certain time when I was in my rented room, and he did just that. He told me when he started his first job and the excitement of being at home with his family and the fact that he couldn't walk anywhere free in his country. Those things made me nostalgic for a life like this. I didn't choose who my father was and shouldn't hide from people threatening to kill me for that, and I shouldn't be a second choice when it came to finding a job. All this Victor was offering me in his letters and inviting me to go and visit his country. He was going to pay for the ticket that was very expensive for me and only a person with a salary like his could afford. I was going to fly to Zuland on the March 13, 1998, and the flight was to Johannesburg, and from there I was going to take a bus for over twelve hours' trip to Harare. I had all the details and ticket in hand for traveling; all I was left to do was to say goodbye to my daughter with a broken heart. I met with her father to let him know of my plans of going away and possibly of not returning back in the near future. I wanted him to have my address in Zuland for contacting me and whenever he wished to write and send me pictures of Luiza. He was more or less interested where I was going and why I was going. He told me that the best thing for me was to get married to some black guy and move on with my life because my daughter was happy where she was, and if I ever thought of having her back, that was never going to happen. Maybe some of it was true, maybe not, but the right thing for me to do was to leave Luiza where she was with a family who could give her what I couldn't, but that wasn't love.

She was six years old and was going to start school in September, and as I held her, she was so relaxed in my arms. Tears were running down my cheeks. I wasn't leaving her forever, and I was going to come back for her one day when the time was right. I wasn't going to do what my mother did to me. I was going to be there for her always even if far away. I was going to stay in touch with her through letters and postcards, and that was when I last saw her before I left Bulgaria. I said very few goodbyes after that with people, and not many others knew that I was leaving the country, not that they were going to notice my absence. I was going away from Lily, and I wanted to leave behind the idea of getting in touch with my family in Angola, perhaps all for the good reasons.

LIFE IN ZULAND

Moving forward with my life was the most important thing, and going away not only to another country but a different continent was going to help me forget the pain of rejection from the people that I loved. I could be anyone in Zuland while in Bulgaria, I was always giving everything without any success. I was twenty-four and wanted to have a stable life, and this was why I was going to Zuland to visit Victor. Also, if I liked the country, I would be able to stay and start afresh. The journey on the plane was very long and took overnight, and the plane was expected to land in the morning around six o'clock. Victor had arranged for a friend of his to meet me at the airport in Johannesburg and take me to his house where I could have some rest throughout the day because the bus to Harare wasn't leaving until ten in the evening. So all the way to his house, his friend stopped at the supermarket to buy me a Coca-Cola and sandwiches that I would carry with me on the bus for my breakfast and lunch the following day. My arrival at Harare was expected around lunchtime, and Victor was going to wait there for me. I didn't get much time to see the city because Victor's friend had to go to work and only had time to drop me at his house and told me that his wife would be home around lunch, and if I wished, both of us could go out for a walk. Then he left for work and I got comfortable on the couch that was big enough for me to lie down, and I fell asleep almost immediately.

The wife came around the time he said she would and prepared some lunch for us and then took me to the local shopping center, which had cinema world, bowling, and many fast-food restaurants. That was when I at last felt comfortable with myself as a person and felt that I belonged in Africa. I could easily fit into the life in Africa and have a job and family, maybe with Victor, and do all these natural things that many around me did to be happy. I really couldn't wait to go to Zuland and see for myself if all the things about the life Victor had told me were true, and if they were, what was there to stop me from achieving what I wanted to? After the walk, I was left amused with the size of the shopping center, the majority of black people that were there with their families and white people everywhere, all sharing tables to eat without any strange looks from either side like everything was all natural to them—a completely normal life, and I felt like I was in heaven where everyone was equal. This is what I wanted from life, an opportunity to have a similar life, and I was hoping that this trip was taking me there.

The time was almost ten, and Victor rang his friend's mobile from Zuland to ensure that everything was okay and I was getting on the bus. The journey was long indeed, and throughout the night I couldn't sleep because I was hypnotized by the stars in the sky and how low they were. It was all so fascinating for me, the whole experience out of Bulgaria for a second time, and this time was going to be for much longer. The thought of leaving my daughter behind always had that bitter taste, and I tried not to think of her much. I wanted her to be happy with her family, and even if eventually I did settle in Zuland, I wasn't sure if I wanted her to live with me. She was about to start school in Pliska, and there was her home. A few times we had to stop the bus for some people to relieve themselves from all the liquids consumed during the journey or for other reasons. Each time the bus had to stop, the lights inside would come on and wake those who were asleep.

Our first stop for rest was around six in the morning and was a place like a motel that had a restaurant, and we all headed straight to it. On the way though, many of us had to stop and follow the noise of excitement that was coming from children screaming near a bush. Surprise! There was a big giraffe eating from the very top of a tree. He wasn't disturbed by the people as though we didn't exist at all. For me, this picture of the giraffe added more pleasure to the fact that I was really in Africa. I had seen one at the zoo in Bulgaria, but I never thought I would see one just like that, free in the nature eating leaves from a tree. God knew what else I was going to see next, and there was something else. Eventually, we carried on and walked toward the restaurant where so many people were gathered together watching something or someone. It was all so natural just to join and watch, so I joined the group. There was a man who had found and killed a meter-and-a-half-long snake. What he was doing with it was interesting to me, as he was removing the skin of the snake and telling the asking people how brave he was to face it. It didn't take him long to remove the skin and then put it in a bag he was wearing across his chest, where he probably stored many more. My English wasn't good at the time, but I did manage to understand that with the remains he was going to treat himself by eating the meat. Just that thought alone put me off eating for the next few hours. After all had their meals and other needs done, we got on the bus to continue with the journey to Zuland.

On my mind was the fear factor of snakes and all other creatures that live free among the people in Africa. I had to have my vaccine against malaria before leaving Bulgaria, as that was one of the applied rules when traveling to Africa without which I wouldn't be able to get a visa. So to be bitten by a mosquito was not my worry. We stopped a few more times and had passed the sign "Welcome to Zuland," and now my anticipation was increasing. I was close, and soon I would meet with Victor and he was the only one now that I could rely on. I didn't know anyone else, and he needed to help me get on with the life in his country and maybe help me find a job.

The bus made a stop at the border of Zuland, where each of us had to queue to have their passports checked and stamped for entering the country. A few were denied entrance, and they were the ones who were transporting stuff to resale and make profit without declaring it. I got there at the end after an hour of waiting and had no problems with my passport as I had no criminal records they could detect on the system, and my passport was stamped. I remained waiting outside near my bus that was attacked by monkeys; they were everywhere! They used the buses for shade because it was a very hot day in Zuland. Even I couldn't stand the heat, and if I was allowed, I would sit inside the bus, but which wasn't to be.

All the buses would be inspected for drugs and other forbidden stuff. Eventually we were ready to drive off, and I couldn't help but notice that half of the bus was empty. Many didn't make it to the capital Harare. The bus pulled up at the main station that was amazingly full with people waiting for its arrival and others waiting to depart. As we stopped and everyone was rushing to get out first and fighting to get their bags, I was trying to capture Victor with my vision, but it was hard. I'd never seen so many black people in one place, and it's been almost six months since I last saw him; surely he wouldn't have changed a lot. I got out of the bus after I picked up my bags on the way out. I didn't have much clothes with me and mainly brought summer clothes, so my bags didn't feel that heavy. Stepping out, I didn't know which direction to take because there was a body of people everywhere and speaking in their local language.

Later, I was told that they were the local equivalent of taxi drivers, only that they were not driving a proper car but something more like a box where you sit and the driver is pulling you as he is cycling. I heard Victor's voice and followed it through the crowd and was relieved to see him again after such a time.

We hugged and then he offered to take the bags from me. To my surprise, his mother was there too with a little boy who happened to be

Victor's nephew. Not that I had something against it, but I was hoping to catch up with Victor first. I smiled and went toward her to give her a hug, but instead she gave me her hand for a shake. Great! I was introduced to Thabiso, the little boy who wasn't very keen to see me as he refused to greet me back. He would've been like six years old. Then Victor exchanged a few words with his mother in their local Ndebele language. We walked to the car park where I learned that Victor had to go back to work as he was unable to get the day off. His mother Eleanor was taking me to the house, and she was going to spend the rest of the day with me until Victor returned later in the evening.

During the journey to the family house, I was sitting in the back of the car and Thabiso was sitting strangely enough on the passenger seat next to Eleanor. She was quiet throughout the journey that seemed long enough for me, and I tried to have conversation with her, only to feel her cold attitude toward me. I tried to talk with Thabiso even though my English wasn't good enough, but all he did was hit me persistently on my knee using his toy. It did hurt, and I thought he did not intend to do it, but then he did it again and laughed with joy the second time. Victor's mother could see what was happening and did nothing. We arrived at the house that was big enough for a whole army, and I could see that the farm they lived in was well looked after. I unloaded my bags and followed Eleanor to the house while being kicked by Thabiso on the way. I didn't know what the problem this child had, but I just ignored him.

Inside the house was nice and organized. Everywhere I looked had flowers and smelled nice. Two women quickly arrived from inside the house, both wearing aprons and gloves on Eleanor's command. They looked at me and smiled with the most genuine smile I have seen that day. They were glad I was there. Eleanor instructed them to take me to my room and then disappeared without saying anything to me. I followed one of the women that helped me carry my bag and talked to herself in the Shona dialect, which is the most spoken dialect in Harare. She obviously didn't speak good English and couldn't communicate with me much, but she smiled a lot. I was brought inside a room that was nice and chilled as it had the ventilator on to keep the room cool. I unpacked my bag and put my clothes on the empty shelves, knowing that Victor wouldn't mind where I put my clothes, and decided to go and find Eleanor and see what her plans were and if she would even show me around. I found her in the kitchen with the cleaning lady that took me to the room, laughing about something, and later learned that her name was Sarah. I joined them and was offered tea and biscuits, which I very much enjoyed. After the tea, Eleanor was going to have a rest and insisted that I do the same until Victor returned from work. I had nothing to say to that; after all, it was her house, but the only problem was I didn't really want to sit in the bedroom for four or five hours. I asked if I could watch TV, and she said only if Thabiso was there too because she wouldn't trust me with the TV controls, which was fair enough.

Later, Thabiso and I were sitting in the lounge. We found something to watch together, and when I was getting into the program, he went and changed it and laughed like it was funny. I wasn't sure what was wrong with that boy, and I gave up and left him alone. I went to have a rest, and before I knew it, I was sleeping. I got woken up by shouting that came from Eleanor. She was upset that I had left Thabiso on his own in the lounge and let him watch any kind of program. I was getting really confused with everything, and before I was able to apologize for what I had done, Eleanor left the room. I just couldn't wait for Victor to be back and talk to him about everything that had happened. I didn't want to create any tension between him and his family, but I felt that I had been abused by his mother and his nephew.

I stayed in my room for the remainder of the day until Victor came back, and before even saying anything to him, I heard his mother's story. I didn't say a word about it and apologized to Eleanor later for the misunderstanding and hoped to get a chance to prove to her that I was not a bad person. That same evening, I met Victor's dad and two brothers who came all the way from town to meet with me, and that was the only time I sat to have a meal with all of them except Wendy, his sister. Victor and I would have dinner separately from then on, and I put it down to his mother not liking me. Victor denied it when I asked him if his mother was upset with me.

I met Thabiso's mother days later only because she was on a business trip to the province, and soon after that, I knew from where Thabiso got it. She was cold to me when we were introduced. I was kind of hoping to become very good friends with her later because we were both of the same age and cared for Victor. She avoided me whenever she could and sometimes wouldn't even say hello when she saw me. So pretty much, my routine was the same every day for months. Victor would go to work early in the morning, and I would stay in bed until lunchtime because that was when everyone would be out to work or visit friends in town. I would find myself alone with the cleaners and mainly Sarah. Sometimes I might have had a sad impression for missing home, and she would come and say a joke or just be around. I know she was making an effort to speak in English, and the little I understood was that her job was even harder than before because Eleanor had fired the second cleaner and Sarah's responsibilities had tripled, but not her salary. In my mind, this was what I call exploitation toward human beings. I did feel sorry for her, and later without realizing that she would get in trouble for that, I told Victor. He told his mother, and then Sarah was forbidden by Eleanor to talk to me. Very rarely I would go outside the farm because they had guard dogs that sometimes were released when none of the residents were at home, but that obviously didn't include me. The dogs didn't know me, and when once I tried to attempt to go out, they jumped on me and Sarah warned me of the serious injuries. I spoke with Victor about that too to have a word with his mother about it. I felt like I was kept as a prisoner, and even if I wished to walk to town, it was miles away and would take me hours each way.

Very rarely on the weekends would Victor take me out to the stadium to watch his favorite team Dynamos playing, and when we got back one time, his mother would shout at him for being late and give me a look that spoke for itself. That would be the very rare occasions to go out when we stayed at his parents' house. Some other weekends she would interfere with our plans for the weekend and have us all spending the day at the Seventh Day Adventist, where she was one of the pastors. I didn't mind going to church, but she forced us to it and it became more like an every Saturday routine. Victor didn't like it, of course, but he was doing it only to avoid seeing her upset. That was how everything was, controlled by her.

One weekday when everyone was at work and I was alone in the house, or so I thought because Sarah had gone for her two hours' break that she was entitled to, I was watching TV in the lounge and could hear crying coming from the house. I first thought that it might be the TV, but it wasn't. I got up from the sofa and walked toward the corridor where my room was. The noise came from the room that was opposite our bedroom. Somebody was there in pain and was calling for help. I pushed the door and found that it was locked. What was going on? Something wasn't right. A person, like a woman's voice, was calling for help and she was locked in. I found Sarah quickly, not even thinking about the dogs for a second. I asked Sarah if she knew where the key was to that room, and she said that the room was locked because Eleanor wished it that way. I insisted that she give me the key and I wouldn't tell Eleanor about it. Sarah had no choice but to give it to me, and I ran straight in the house to unlock the bedroom door. I found an old African woman inside suffering from the pain and maybe the humiliation to have been found pissing on the floor. I had never met her before, and there she lived under the same roof as me. Sarah followed me in to see if I needed any help, which I did. I helped her change the wet clothes this old woman was wearing and the sheets she slept on which I could tell hadn't been changed for days. We replaced them and placed her back in bed. She had that smile of gratitude on her face for what we did, and it gave me no less pleasure to see her comfortable and dry. She asked for an additional pillow, and then I learned this new word. I told Sarah to keep this between us and I knew she would because she herself wasn't satisfied with the money she was paid, and on top of that, she was supposed to bathe the poor woman twice a week among the hundred tasks she already had.

I learned from her that the old woman's name was Jenny and she was the mother-in-law of Eleanor, who wasn't pleased to have her in the house and had ignored her since she has been there. Obviously, the second cleaner would have been the one to look after Jenny and take her out for to sit under the sun, but when she left, things had changed. I spoke with Victor about it and asked him if it was okay to look after his grandmother while they were all out and working. He didn't mind and spoke with his mother about it too. I knew she wouldn't have minded but for the fact that I was helping with something in the house and she felt uncomfortable. Many times before, when I offered to help her in the kitchen, like cutting onions or peeling potatoes, she would have a reason to decline my help. She couldn't stand me, and that was obvious to me from the very first time we met. Sometimes when Wendy came for a visit on the weekends she would offer the same help and Eleanor would allow her to do it. I was living there under the same roof for months with her and still I didn't know what to do for her to like me.

Caring after her mother-in-law wasn't something I wanted her to like me for because this was something humans do for each other. I never even asked her why Jenny's room was locked. Now I had meaning to my days and even more someone to share them with when Victor was at work. Jenny was in her eighties and was sick from something that I never got to understand what exactly. I would visit her room every day before she was moved to a hospital eventually. I would feed her breakfast and listen to her talking in Shona (local language in Zuland, mainly spoken in the territory of Mashonaland), which I didn't understand and she probably knew that, yet she often smiled at me. I just cared about her and held her on the way to the bathroom, where I gave her a bath and then dressed her. Later, if it was nice and hot outside, we would sit there and sometimes Sarah would join us there too. The two of them would speak in Shona, and Sarah would struggle to translate to me. Jenny wanted to know about me, and I told her about my past. She would smile and hold my hand for some time, then when it got cold, we would go back in and I'd help her sit in the lounge with me and watch TV. Sometimes Eleanor would arrive from work before Victor and would sit in the lounge to talk with Jenny only and ask her if she was feeling fine and not bother asking me the same. Victor would be happy to come from work and talk with his grandmother and have a joke where she would laugh. I was enjoying these moments with her around.

One day, Victor came from work with a newspaper in his hand excited to show me something inside, and I was excited when I saw it too. It was a pool competition organized by some pub. I was nervous and unsure whether to do it or not, but Victor encouraged me to do it, and the next day when he got back from work, we went together to the shopping center in West Gate, mainly a place where the white people do their shopping. I got the chance to choose my own cue stick for the very first time. It was a quality one; soon after I held it, I knew it was the one. Victor paid for it, and I promised to pay him back when I won the tournament, as a joke more or less. Days later, he took me to the place where the tournament would be held so that I'd have a go on the tables and get the feeling before the competition. The place had about ten pool tables and surely was suited for tournaments. For the next few days, I would go on my own after Victor had shown me the way to get to town and back to the house. Victor also warned me to be careful and not to trust people and to avoid asking anyone for directions. It became like a routine for me to go on my own to town and quickly learned the area I was visiting. I took part in the first pool tournament, and I guess I overestimated myself because I got all the way to the finals only to lose. I was the only woman, and not just that, but the only colored woman to be involved. I would've not noticed something like that if it wasn't mentioned to me after the tournament was over. I guess in Zuland, women didn't go public and play pool with men. The culture was more conservative when it came to that, but I was seen as an attraction to the organizers of the tournament, and I assured them that my involvement in the pool competition had only just begun in Zuland and I wished to continue. So from that moment on, I would go to town and practice for every weekend tournament. Victor's mother didn't find that very amusing, but it wasn't down to her to tell me what to do with my time off. I still looked after Jenny whenever I could, and she was always happy to see me. I was playing for a few hours only and then came back to the house before dusk, and nobody ever noticed my absence.

One day after I had finished practice, I decided to wander around for a bit because I had plenty of time before my bus when I saw the flag. It was the embassy of my father's country on the flag, and it was not very far from where I played pool. I was surprised to have come across it in Harare, and Victor never mentioned there having one. The question was if I should go in or not. I passed it and then walked back and then passed it again. I was still deciding what to do when the guard came out of the building and asked me if I was lost. I thanked him for trying to help and then asked him if I could see somebody at the embassy and didn't tell him more. He went in and, after a short while, appeared, asking me to follow him. I had to leave my document at his desk. I followed him to the second floor on the elevator and got invited to sit in an empty office. I waited for about ten minutes, and in the meantime as on the table in front of me were lots of magazines from my father's country, all written in Portuguese, I took one and turned over the pages while waiting. My eyes stopped on a photograph of my father, and I couldn't believe what I was seeing. The picture of my father I had seen many times, but the mark which he had on his upper lip was identical to the one I have. I couldn't take my eyes off it. It was a birthmark for sure; this can't be coincidence that I have the same spot on my lip as my father and the same gap between my teeth. The woman who worked at the office walked in while I was holding the magazine and introduced herself. She wasn't a person whose name I would remember. She sat comfortably enough to listen to my reasons for being at the embassy when most of the personnel was on holiday, including the ambassador.

I told her that my father was the late president of her country and I wished to speak with someone who could help me on the matter. She asked me if I was in Zuland for the same reason, and I told her that I was visiting a friend who was Zulandan. She said that there was a person who could help me and her name was Mrs. Luisa Chongolola and that she would be back the next week.

I thanked her for having the time to see me and left. I missed my bus and had to wait for the next one. I got back safe, and all I could think of was the image of my father I saw at the embassy's magazine. I told Victor everything when he got back from work, and he maybe resented that. He told me that it wasn't worth dealing with these people, especially as they had me over all these years and they had done nothing for me, which was true. However, one thing Victor wouldn't understand was that I wasn't doing this only for me but for my daughter and her children one day too. Not only that, but my father knew about my existence and wanted me, but due to the circumstances, I ended up in an orphanage. He died not having that chance to see me, and it was not down to the family to deny me the right as his daughter. I wrote a letter with Victor's help to Mrs. Chongolola and had it ready when I was meeting her to give it to her. The days turned into a week, and before I knew it, I was at the embassy waiting to be seen by Mrs. Chongolola herself and she knew who I was and what she would be dealing with.

It was May 1998 and I was sitting with Victor in the lobby waiting, and we were either early or she was late. When she finally arrived, though we had never even met, she walked toward me with a smile and hugged me like we were long-lost friends! I thought that the behavior was a bit strange since I didn't know the person, but later it was explained to me that I looked so much like one of the children of my father that she was confused. Anyway, only I could go inside the office and was welcomed to sit. Mrs. Chongolola read the letter that I had given her and then heard my story from me and was determined to help me. She informed me that she would phone Mrs. Irene and Mrs. Ruth, both sisters of my late father, that same day and she would come back to me after that. She did call me a few days later at the house and asked me to bring to the embassy a copy of my birth certificate and as many pictures as I could because she needed to send them to the family. I did that in a matter of hours after she sent the driver from the embassy to the house to pick me up. Jenny was sitting outside in the sun with me when the driver arrived. She wanted to know what it was about, and I told her it had to do with my father's family and then she smiled and said that everything would be okay and they will come for me sooner than I thought. I wished that her words would come true and I believed her even though I was in the same situation before when they asked for my pictures and did nothing. I had to have faith and believe it this time.

I was at Mrs. Chongolola's office giving her in person the required pictures and copy of my document, and I told her that I didn't believe anything would happen and I wouldn't hear a word from his family. She insisted that this time they would come, but they needed to see my pictures first and birth certificate to see if I have any resemblance to the person that I claimed to be my father. The birth certificate they would use to compare with dates of his traveling to Eastern Europe or Bulgaria in particular. Anyway, I had nothing to lose but to see what would happen after that, and having been greatly disappointed by the neglect toward me shown by the family and the country, I wasn't going to let them affect my life or wait for the phone to ring. Eleanor, in the meantime, wanted Victor to move out of the house and find his own place with me. That wasn't hard, and in a week's time, we moved out and friends of Victor helped us with transporting our stuff.

That was more like it for both of us, having our own space and independence around the place. His parents were invited to come and visit us whenever they wanted, but they never did. Victor and I continued visiting them at the farm on the Saturdays after church and have a family lunch together. Eleanor's behavior toward me hadn't changed, and sometimes she would ring Victor on his mobile to tell him not to bother coming as one of his brothers would bring food for him on the way to town. That probably did hurt Victor, but he never showed it to his parents or even me. I continued playing pool and taking part in the competitions and did win one of the tournaments eventually, and my popularity was growing among the pool world in Zuland. Most players were scared to bet against me because my style of play was very direct and aggressive to what they were used to. I wasn't thinking where the time had gone since I arrived in March, and with Victor to that point, we had never discussed the possibility of a future together but surely he had it in mind because he proposed to me one day and I didn't have to think too much and said yes. After all, he did make me happy, and

I could see my future with him in Zuland. I left it for Victor to inform his family about our plans, and only Sarah and Jenny truly congratulated us one afternoon when we were over at the farm. The wedding date was decided as for July 24, 1998, in the Harare registrar, nothing fancy like a big wedding celebration, only a small group of very close friends and family of Victor, and that is if he got his way to have it at the farm.

In between, I was invited to join the snooker club of the Reserve Bank of Harare. One of the pool players who was called Tendai on the weekend competitions liked me and approached me after the match with a serious offer and opportunity to play for the county. He told me that with my good eye for the game, I could make a good snooker player. He also explained that one of their teammates had left the team, and without the third person, the team would be disqualified from the league. I thought about it because snooker was nothing like pool. The size of the table was twice as big and the balls smaller and the pocket tighter. It was hard to make a rational decision, and I promised to visit the club during one of the match sessions against the opponent and make my decision then. I needed to feel the table and the balls. The cue stick I already had was perfect for snooker, and the tip of my cue was 9mm, which made it perfect for the game. Victor joined me at the club where we watched a game of snooker between the two teams, but it wasn't that impressive as both players were unable to pot easy balls over the pockets and extended the game up to an hour. At the end, I was able to establish that if you are good potter, you will certainly be able to play the game, but I didn't want only to be able to pot the balls. I wanted to be able to make big breaks and win the game in one or two visits at the table. I committed myself to play snooker for the club, but only from the new season because I wanted to prepare and train so that I could be up to standard when I competed. Tendai and the captain of the team, Francis, agreed with me, and I was going to join them when the new season started in March 1999.

One day, I received a phone call through Victor's mobile, and it was his mother saying that someone from the embassy was looking for me and I needed to go there soon as possible, if not in the next hours, then the following day. I phoned the embassy from a pay phone and asked to speak with Mrs. Chongolola, who was already expecting my call and urgently said that I must come to the embassy immediately because someone was in the country to meet with me. I wasted no more time and got into the first taxi to town with Victor next to me. I had no idea who that might be and could only guess. I got there, and Victor was told that he couldn't go with me where I was going. Everything was kept such a secret from others, but surely I was going to tell Victor later on. Anyway, he was upset not to be where I was since I was his responsibility in the country and he didn't trust the embassy people and tried to implement theories of my kidnapping. I wasn't scared for a second where they might be taking me, and Mrs. Chongolola was sitting next to me in the embassy car telling me that soon everything would be over and I would get the chance to meet a person who was also related to my father's family.

We arrived at the compound of expensive houses and walked toward the house. The driver pulled the car on the side to wait for us. It must have been around three or four in the afternoon when Mrs. Chongolola pressed the doorbell hard enough to ring and a man opened the door wide to the house. They exchanged hugs and a few words, and then his attention was focused on me. The first words he ever said were "Hi, Lucy! It is a pleasure to meet with you and I hope that this won't be our last meeting. I am the deputy foreign minister, and I was a very close friend to your father. He invited me inside, and Mrs. Chongolola returned to the car as I went inside the house. I was surprised that it was only me and the foreign minister alone, and I have to say that the thought of something happening to me crossed my mind. However, he didn't give me any sign of being a man of violence, and when he sat down on a chair, I followed him too. He said that he was being sent to talk to me first by the family and get to know a few more details of my past. I asked him a direct question, and that was if he thought that I was the daughter of the late president. He smiled and said, "The pictures of you had brought me here, but the family want to know a little bit more about you and your life. We spent hours talking, and it wasn't until I found it late and time to go that we separated. He told me that he would meet with me again soon and then he phoned the embassy. The time must have been around six in the evening when Mrs. Chongolola came with the embassy car and took me home. Victor was waiting patiently for me, although he didn't like the fact that I was gone so long and he was almost going to call the police. I told him everything about my meeting with the deputy foreign minister and how he could see the resemblance with my father. Victor said not to get carried away when nothing has been done for me yet.

The time for the marriage ceremony was drawing near, and Victor still hadn't heard from his parents if we could use the farm for the wedding party or not. I was upset with the fact that Jenny was in a hospital and her situation had drastically worsened since I last saw her, and sometimes I blamed myself for not being there to look after her. I could imagine her being left in her wet sheets and not having a bath for weeks and locked in her room. Perhaps it was for her best to be in a hospital and cared for. I was told that she was asking to see me, and Victor and I decided to do it one Saturday after church. We all went there to visit her; she was so weak, yet she did manage to say my name in a whisper. I stood there feeling that this might be the end of the road for her, and it wasn't far from the truth. She died that same afternoon hours after we visited her.

I lost a friend and perhaps the grandmother that I never had. I knew she would have wanted me to be happy with Victor. We buried her in her village of birth, and the ceremony was spectacular in an African traditional way: a cow was sacrificed in her name and celebrated in dance around the fire until late.

Days later, Victor and I were at the registrar waiting for our names to be called. The only person that had shown up for our ceremony was Wendy, Victor's sister. Victor wasn't happy at all, and I did feel for him; after all, he was the firstborn child and they showed disrespect toward him in that way on a day that mattered to him the most. The ceremony went through quickly as we arrived and then we all went our separate ways. Wendy went back to work, and Victor told me only after that he had to go to work and I was greatly disappointed in the fact that the whole thing was a big disappointment! What a way to start my married life! Despite Victor trying to hide his emotions and the disappointment that his parents didn't show up, he couldn't hide his drinking, which was increasing every day. It was getting harder and harder to talk to him about anything, so getting myself involved in practicing snooker helped me escape the already troubled marriage. Victor's mother was avoiding him, and that hurt him a lot as well as our marriage. Sometimes he would stay at work for as long as he could and the following day I would find that he hadn't been home and had not even called me. I became very lonely too, and only snooker and the pool tournaments kept me going. Victor would still come and watch me play snooker, but only if there was something to drink. Sometimes I wouldn't be able to finish my game of pool in a tournament because he would pass out unconscious on the floor and I would have to take care of him. For a week or two, I avoided going there to save myself from embarrassment of what he did.

It was around November 1998 when I received another call from the embassy and Mrs. Chongolola. Nothing had been said over the phone, and I was hoping that whatever it was would finally put an end to the long saga. I was taken by the embassy car, and Mrs. Chongolola stayed with me. We stopped in front of a very posh villa that had a swimming pool. The door was opened soon after we arrived as though we were expected. The person was looking through the window every other second. Mrs. Chongolola walked in front of me and was greeted first by a woman with whom she exchanged many kisses. The woman didn't say anything to me and stepped back to her previous position. I could see that the room was filled with people, yet none greeted me. Mrs. Chongolola was then hugged by another woman whom she introduced soon after to me. "Lucy, I would like you to meet Mrs. Ruth!" She was the sister of my late father.

My legs went soft, and I approached her with my hand out to take hers and looked into her eyes as I said, "It is an honor to meet you, Mrs. Ruth." I waited for her to say something, but she didn't. She looked as if she had seen a ghost. She excused herself and went upstairs to my surprise. I thought nothing of it then and was offered to sit on the couch beside Mrs. Chongolola. Four or five of the women in the room I wasn't introduced to were staring at me and speaking in Portuguese. I wasn't sure what was going on and who would eventually break the news to me whatever that was. Then somebody called my name and I recognized his voice; it was the deputy foreign minister. He was always charming with me and perhaps there was a reason for that. He said how lovely it was to see me again and that he kept his promise to meet with me again. We went upstairs, just me and him and found Mrs. Ruth sitting by herself on the terrace having a drink. I was thinking how inappropriate her behavior was to leave me downstairs and come up here, but later I understood the reasons for that.

As I sat across the table, I could have a very good view of Mrs. Ruth. She had the same birthmark on her upper lip, and in fact, looking at her closely, I could see some glimpses of myself, but only of an older version. She was nervous that it was obvious, so she let the deputy talk while she was observing me carefully. Mrs. Ruth was asking the questions in Portuguese, and the foreign minister was translating them to me. The questions were the same that I was asked on our previous meeting and I had thought completely irrelevant. There was a reason for Mrs. Ruth to come all the way from her country with the whole delegation sent by the president.

The meeting lasted more or less an hour, and the main point that we reached by the suggestion of Mrs. Ruth was that we should do a DNA test to determine if I was the daughter as I claimed to be or not. Mrs. Ruth promised to introduce me to the whole family if I was proved to be the daughter, of course, without any hesitation. She would arrange the DNA test with the family to take place in a month's time. We were not over yet although I was asked to go downstairs and wait, which I did, and left them both to have a private conversation. Mrs. Chongolola thought that it was time to go, only for Mrs. Ruth to appear and hand her a significant amount of money rolled in a ball, which Mrs. Chongolola passed to me but I refused to take, saying that I was fine without it. This was how I met my aunt, Mrs. Ruth, a likeable person whom I was very unfortunate not to know. I didn't know what to think of her visit to Zuland, and who were the other people in the room that I wasn't introduced to? What was the point of them being there when all I had to do was talk to Mrs. Ruth and the foreign minister? I was to wait and see with time what would happen, but in the meantime, I was happy to have agreed to have a DNA test and, finally, everything looked promising. I was taken back home by the embassy car, excited to share the news with Victor, but he wasn't there. There was no note, nothing. I understood that he was getting sick and tired with the whole family recognition, but this was part of my life that he needed to understand, that in order for me to be complete, I had to prove the truth about myself.

I continued practicing snooker and trained alongside Tendai and Francis. My game was shaping up, and the understanding of the rules helped me win occasional games against them. They sometimes tried to convince me that I was left to win, but I wasn't so sure about that, at least not all the time. Victor joined me for practice sometimes and learned how to play himself, but he wasn't as good as me though he still enjoyed the competition every now and then. After that, when we'd finish with the snooker, we'd sit at the bar in the club and watch the Premier League matches, something Victor liked to do, or watch any other sport that was on. It did help him a lot to socialize with Tendai and Francis, and they became friends with time. Tendai and I would be playing in the pool competition on the weekends, and often he got beaten halfway through and if I didn't get to the final, at least I won the third or fourth prize and would then buy Tendai and Victor a beer. Francis never joined us in the competition because he believed that his snooker game would be affected by the pool with the different angles and pockets. Anyway, that didn't stop Tendai and me playing pool every week.

With time, I noticed that Victor became more relaxed and happy. I guess he had found a way to forgive his parents, and we started visiting them on a weekly basis again. His parents had a plan to open a pub inside the farm, which Victor thought was a strange idea, given the fact that this would attract many drunk people to their house late at night. That wasn't Victor's decision to make, and the plans of having a pub went ahead. Victor's knowledge was used when it came to the electricity and cables fitting; he was put in charge, and the work he did in the farm was well appreciated by Eleanor. She was having her son back, that was for sure, because as it turned out, Victor spent most of his time after work helping with the building and completely neglected me as part of his life. I would go and visit him at the farm in the afternoons just to be close to him and maybe help, but that wasn't appreciated by Eleanor and she would often tell me that Victor was busy and I could wait for him inside the house. I would wait until it was ten in the evening, sometimes even later, sitting and watching TV, waiting for him to come and see me. Surely he would want something to eat or drink at one point, and what was actually happening was his mother wouldn't even bother telling him that I was in the house. That would lead later to misunderstanding and arguments. I told Victor later that I didn't feel good going to his parents' house because I was not treated well and would rather stay at home, pointing out to him the time we spent together. That was when he told me that his first priority was his family, by which he meant his mother! It was like I was being hit with a wet towel across the face. I didn't think he meant that, but his actions spoke clearly for themselves and he continued putting his mother first in everything: for example, if I wanted us to do something on the weekend, he'd say, "Sorry, I can't. My mother asked me if I can do this . . ." And that was how our marriage was run—by his mother and her desires.

I received the papers that gave me the right to work in the country and decided to do something about it. Since I was without a profession, I thought it was better to obtain one; and in January 1999, I registered to study cosmetology at Dudley's for two years and become a hairdresser. I knew that this was going to be a massive challenge for me because the subject itself was hard when it comes to learning about the components and the chemical reactions of the products involved in the industry, and my English level wasn't as good to really even qualify. I became a student and attended all my lessons from nine till five Monday to Friday. Victor was happy with that decision because he thought that being a hairdresser was a very prestigious job in Zuland and paid well. There was another aspect that was in my favor, and that was my skin color. I never thought that in Zuland people would discriminate my color or the black people for that matter, especially that they lived in their own country. However, that was the ugly truth in the country and now I should consider myself special and obligated to do things after the white people.

In my group, we were like twenty women and most of them coming from the poor rural areas of the capital city. I have to say they didn't get on well with me for being colored, and I totally understood that. I wanted to be part of the group and couldn't because I was rejected. I found my homework much harder to understand and got Victor to find me a Bulgarian dictionary and started translating everything and then reading it. It was very hard to do it on my own without someone helping me. At school, I sat on the front row so that I could listen and understand what the teacher was telling us, which was the theory of the hair. We'd have lunch break for one hour, and each one of us would go to the canteen for a nice cooked meal. I'd follow the group like an outsider because I was the only colored among them and felt uncomfortable. They used to make jokes about me and the white people that they have met. Funny, I was thinking, how in my home country Bulgaria I was black "Negro" and here the blacks don't consider me black but white because of my white genes. I'd sit on my own and have lunch and then go back on my own to the classroom, waiting to continue with the lesson.

One evening, I woke up very cold like somebody had locked my body in a freezer for hours. I pushed Victor and told him to give me more blankets, which he did. My body then went boiling, and it was like nothing I have ever experienced before. Tons of sweat and wet clothes was all I could remember. My body reached over forty degrees, and I was totally unconscious. Victor took me to one of his aunties that luckily for me owned a small pharmacy and she was able to figure out that I had malaria and needed medicine immediately. For the next days, despite taking my prescriptions on a regular basis, I continued to lose weight and it was nothing like the previous me. I looked like a dead woman walking. The clothes I had were no more in use or kept for later when I gained my kilos back. My condition didn't look very good, and I lost the appetite to eat and my food was mainly smoothies and fruits. I resumed my cosmetology class, and if I had troubles to cope with the material back then, now was even harder.

One of the girls in the class, maybe because she felt sorry for me or because later she told me that one of her distant relatives was white, gave me help with coping in class so now I had a companion at the college. Her name was Cleona, and she became my buddy. With her, I could share things that bothered me, like my marriage and stuff. She was married herself with two little boys, and her husband was colored, not that the other women in the class knew. Then she explained to me the segregation that this country still lived in. The whites had a better standard of living, then the colored people, who also, like the whites, had a good standard of living and good jobs and had isolated themselves from the whites and the blacks. At the bottom was the native blacks of whom the majority had no education and jobs. So a person like me after graduation would take the job from the black person. This is why the women from the class didn't like me. I was a threat to their chances of finding a job more or less. Surely life wasn't fair for any of the black people, and the majority were pushed to extremes of stealing and killing even.

I was still waiting for news from the embassy regarding the DNA test that should have been arranged by that time and contacted Mrs. Chongolola to find if she had any news for me, but there was nothing. Every other week when I called her, she would say, "Better wait," which seemed to be her favorite phrase for weeks. I waited, of course, what else could have I done? I have waited for years and surely could wait for a few more weeks, but knowing that if you give them time to do something, they will never do it. So I decided not to wait anymore because I'd been waiting from November 1998 until April 1999. I contacted a journalist from the *Daily News* in Harare and told him I had a story. He, of course, warned me of the impact the story might have on the government in concern and I said that I had done this before in Bulgaria and was threatened to be killed by many and wasn't scared of dying. The journalist's name was Lloyd Mudiwa, and he took the story with passion and without a fear.

The story was published on April 22, 1999, on the same page next to the one of Y sir 'Araf t's visit to Harare. The story obviously came as a shock to many people who worked at the embassy, including Mrs. Chongolola herself. I told her that I needed to do something in order to get the attention of the family and the Angolan government too. I thought that it was disgraceful the way I was neglected for years by them, and although I have overreacted, to some extent, what did they expect from someone raised in an institution and lacking class? Anyway, everyone got to see the story and everyone who commented praised my courage. Well, I did it! And now I was going to wait for their reaction, which in fact came five months later. This time I was to travel to Pretoria in South Africa for a DNA test. I was going to travel on my own to South Africa and be met by the deputy foreign minister. However, there was a problem for me to obtain a visa for the day I was expected to travel. That was when everyone else involved with the DNA test from the family was in Pretoria waiting for my arrival.

I wasn't yet a citizen of my father's country, and I didn't work for the embassy who was trying desperately to obtain a visa for me in the next twenty-four hours. I was told to lie to the consul when I attended a brief interview at the embassy of South Africa, that my father was a Mr. Rocha who worked for the embassy in South Africa and he was critically ill. I don't know if he believed all this, but it worked in the end. I was going to travel under a false name as a daughter of the Mr. Rocha, and the passport I was going to use was under the name of that other person. Mrs. Chongolola was waiting for me in the lobby, and after we got my passport visa, I was taken straight to the airport by the embassy car with Mrs. Chongolola next to me. She was running the show on behalf of somebody else, and they wanted me on the first possible plane to South Africa. We had time to wait for the plane and sat in a cafe.

The whole thing had been very strange the way it was rushed and having to lie to an official. Mrs. Chongolola was a nice person, and I could tell she wanted this case over with. She gave me a note of $100 to spend while I was in Pretoria and wished me good luck with the DNA. She said she believed that I was indeed the daughter of my father and really wished the best for me. Minutes later, I was on the plane to South Africa for an hour or two, and there waiting was the deputy foreign minister. He took the passport from me to look after it. We sat in the back of a car and drove through Johannesburg. The journey felt longer to me than the flight, but I didn't mind at all. I was looking forward to giving blood for the DNA test and for a positive outcome.

We arrived in Pretoria around dusk, and the room I was given was a whole apartment with luxury. Mr. Romao came and knocked on my door and invited me out for dinner. I was concerned that I haven't the appropriate dress for going out in the posh area, but he smiled and said, "You can choose the food." We went out on a main lively area with hundreds of restaurants and coffee shops, and I picked an Italian restaurant because I was familiar with the food. I had my favorite dish of spaghetti carbonara and he had steak with chips.

I remember him offering me to try the meat, and I told him that I didn't like meat but did get some of his chips. We mainly discussed the country's politics and he talked about my father and what a great man he was for the country. He asked me what I intended to do in case I did turn out to be the daughter of the late president. I said I wanted to study law and become a lawyer, a fair one! We had a laugh, and I could tell he was so relaxed there was no tension on the table. We got back to the hotel to our respective rooms, and I was really tired after the long day and went to bed.

We had planned breakfast for the following day, but there was no sign of the deputy. I went to the reception, and the woman told me to go ahead and have breakfast and that I should expect him to be back before ten o'clock. As I sat in the restaurant having my breakfast, the woman from the reception came to me and said that there was a phone call from a woman called Mrs. Ruth and if I would like to speak with her. I took the phone from her and talked to my aunt. She wanted to know where the deputy was as she was trying to reach him in his room for hours. Unfortunately, I was asking myself the same question. I gave the phone back to the receptionist and continued with my breakfast. An hour later, I was wandering around the shops waiting for the deputy to appear from somewhere. I had just bought myself a perfume So, and there he was behind me! He said he had been looking for me, but his mood was different today from the way he was talking. He was nervous about something; I noticed that something was bothering him and that could have been me possibly, but I was trying not to think about it.

We rushed everything that day, the second of September. He hadn't asked me how I'd slept or how I was for that matter either. He took me to the clinic straight away, and I gave blood almost as soon as I got in there. They said the results would be ready within a month and be sent to us. Then he rushed us back to the hotel to pay whatever he owed and got in the car to go straight to the airport without a word. He was making me nervous with his presence, and I remember thinking that it might have had something to do with the call from Mrs. Ruth that day. He dropped me at the airport and finally enlightened me. "You have to go on your own now. There are people who want to harm you, and it's easy to find you if I am around you. Somebody was supposed to take care of you." Then he disappeared.

That was the third and last time when I met with the deputy foreign minister of my father's country. It was in my belief that he did what he was told but at the same time he liked me; I could tell by the way he was relaxed with me at the restaurant and talked about everything. Somebody was supposed to "take care of me," in what sense had he said that? I don't know! I wasn't dwelling on that too much and headed toward the information desk to get information on my next flight to Zuland. I had just about an hour before departure as passengers were queuing for check-in, when the strangest thing happened—I found that I didn't have the passport with me, the one I arrived to South Africa with and was being asked to show in order to have my ticket stamped and validated. The airport was huge, and I was unable to find the deputy. I was in panic because it was serious. I had to go back to Zuland, and the only way was to call Victor. With the money that Mrs. Chongolola gave me, I called Victor at his workplace and asked him to leave work to find a Xerox and fax a copy of my passport to the airport in South Africa. Not only that, but he had to buy me the return ticket. He met me at the airport and was furious with the way I was left on my own at the airport as anything could have happened to me. I was just happy to be back with him safe and sound. I went to see Mrs. Chongolola a few days later and told her about my disappointment of being left behind by the deputy; she had nothing to say but reassured me that everything would be fine for me but I must be patient. Now that the hard part was done, which was to go to Pretoria and give blood, I should take it easy and wait for the results, which was true.

So the results I was expecting was around the beginning of October 1999, and they would have been sent to me at my address in Harare. Every day from that month I'd be checking my mail, and even Victor himself was excited about the DNA results. It was all I could think of, yet October passed without a letter from the Medgene Diagnostic Laboratories CC. I visited the embassy many times to find out if Mrs. Chongolola had any information from her sister-in-law and my aunt Mrs. Ruth, but she never had. They kept her in the dark, and she told me that they had forbidden her to make any contact with me and to deny me access regarding this matter. But she was kind to me as always and wished me all the best with my persuasion of proving the truth. She was worried that each time I was there to see her, someone from the embassy would report her back home to the government and she might get in trouble, but she was only trying to help.

By November, I still didn't have any news on the DNA results; and on November 11, 1999, which also happened to be the national day of Angola, I phoned the clinic in Pretoria while I was on a lunch break at the college and asked to speak with the person in charge. I was finally on the phone with somebody who knew about my results but was unwilling to give them to me either over the phone or even when I requested posting. I was furious about it and said that I was going to have a lawyer involved if he refused to mail them to me. He said that only the family was entitled to have the results since they had paid for them, but he was going to phone them and ask their permission to have them sent to me. We agreed that he would phone me later that day with the answer. I gave him my mobile number to call me, which he did a few hours later when I was in the middle of class and had to excuse myself and go out. He asked me where to send the results, and over the phone, I gave him my address.

A week later, I received them but had no heart to open the letter, which I carried for a few days before I did, thinking over the last month or so that something wasn't right. The results were ready, yet nobody from the family had contacted me and not only that, they didn't want me to have them. I had to practically scare the poor man with a lawyer to have them sent to me. I did open the letter and went through it carefully, and at the bottom of it was the verdict that "no conclusion could be reached" as to whether or not he was my biological father. Of course, the main character that was supposed to be on that DNA piece of paper was Mrs. Ruth herself and she wasn't there. Very clever! They had the mother, Maria, with two of her children for that matter and all they could establish was that Maria is not my mother so therefore couldn't tell if her children had the same father as me. How stupid the whole thing looked when I shared it with a professor from the Cambridge University years later. Of course, in the case of a deceased father, you can use the blood samples from his brothers and sister to determine relationship, something obviously done on purpose. It was a major disappointment for me, the whole thing and the results. It was clear to me as a white day that it was in someone's interest not to recognize me and in fact they had the real results, which they did not like. Why else come up with something like a "no conclusions" result if not to attempt to cover the truth? Totally opposite would have been if I wasn't the daughter of the late president. I would have heard all about it and was charged for false allegations and conspiracy of trying to damage his image, using his image in publications, and so on. They were quiet; in fact, nobody tried to contact me and say, "Lucy, we are not happy of the outcome either, so let's do another one elsewhere," but no. They were certainly happy, and in fact, later I learned that the results they had given to the president were in fact "negative." Now this could have been a reason for investigation, but who cares? I had different results obviously to the ones they "had," and nobody questioned that.

I sent a copy of mine to Mrs. Chongolola and spoke with her over the phone because I didn't want her to be seen helping me and get in trouble. I asked her to send a letter to Mrs. Ruth that I had written with the desire to visit Angola and have a conversation with her, but there was no result. I tried to contact the deputy foreign minister, but he was also unavailable all the times when I phoned his office, which continued for months. I gave up for a while, convincing myself that they would contact me one day soon.

I focused my attention in March 2000 on my first season as a snooker player at the Reserve Bank Sports Club. My first tournament was a small women's competition that was going to give me the test of the challenge in the game. I got beaten by a woman call Sandy Jacobs. She was the best female snooker player in Zuland, and for the last five seasons, no other woman had managed to win the competition. She was a tough player who understood the safety part of the game and used it well. As for me, I was just going for the shots aiming to pot as many balls to get the points, but if I missed, I was increasing her chances of winning the game. So Sandy won that year's women tournament and I believe I had finished second from the bottom. Not so exciting, but that was how my love for snooker began. I was still visiting my college and in the evenings would have a match. Usually if Victor wasn't at home before the game, I'd be picked up by Francis from my place and then if we were the visiting team we'd order drinks on the house. We waited until everyone gathered, and then the captain of the team would select with the opposite captain which players would play each other. Each player would play two games with two different players from the opposite team. I remember playing without a fear and winning my first game, which was the opening game of the match. Nobody expected me to win my first game in the league, but I did it and that gave the sound for the remainder of the season: out of the thirty-six games I had played, I lost only three, and that helped the team to win the league for the first time and from Mashonaland D division, the team was promoted to Mashonaland C division. I have also entered in the individual single competition for the D division, which I had won.

I became like the lucky charm for the all black team, and we competed throughout the season against teams who were mainly white Zulandans with English, Dutch, German heritage. The team had the leader, and that was me. I was winning my first game each time to motivate the rest, and they just followed me. At the end of the season in October was the prize ceremony, and my team was up there to lift our first trophy and captain Francis Motungama was a very proud man. I received my individual and team prize, but one I was still going for was the ladies' singles that was weeks later. I won my three games in the group conveniently and was against Sandy

Jacobs in the final. I beat Sandy under the eyes of her teammates, friends, and supporters. The venue where we played the competition was her venue, and not one black person was in the room to watch, simply because they were not allowed without permission unless they were playing in the tournament. So I did it! I won the ladies' single 2000, and all the trophies I had won that year I dedicated to the Reserve Bank Sports Club.

In the meantime at college, we had moved onto the practical part of the course and I was practicing hairstyles on a dummy taken from the manual. I wasn't the best in the class and often stayed behind the others for some additional training. It was the end of the theory year for us, and next year we'd all be out there doing it for real. I know most of the girls were far better than me and stood a better chance of getting the job. Most of us would easily get a year's job from any hairdresser salon if we only mentioned that we were from Dudley's. I found myself a place to work for a year, and it was near where Cleona lived and she probably did help me by getting me there. She herself decided to do it from home so that she could be near her kids; besides, it wasn't an uncommon practice in Zuland. So in the following year 2001, I quickly adapted to the new working place and accepted it, perhaps maybe because my boss was colored and the other hairdressers were colored too. I had to get up much earlier this time because two transports were required and often in the mornings in Harare town you'd need to give a good fight to get into the minibus that would only fit in eight to ten if someone was breathing down the driver's neck! I'd get in as early appointments as nine, almost as soon as I arrived and without a first cup of coffee to kick my day. Most of my customers were women to shampoo and conditioning then gentle drying before gel was applied, and from there the senior hairdresser handled them for a professional hairstyle and I would be on to the next one.

I would finish in the afternoon and then go home straight from work and prepare dinner for Victor, whom I would rarely see. Since the opening of the pub, he spent more and more time up there than coming home. He had found a new hobby and that was to be a bartender, and he did it for nothing so as to help the business make some profit. I just didn't understand why he had to do that job when he had his two brothers who were jobless and with no responsibilities at the time and a job like that would have been good for them, but of course because they were young, like in their early twenties, all they did was go clubbing all night. But that was his parents' problem to solve without having to interfere in our marriage.

Many times I'd talk with Victor about the importance of going away just the two of us to start again. It had been almost three years since we were married and with no future planned because everything was put on hold for his parents' pub. I was feeling miserable, and also the times I had sent letters to my daughter in Bulgaria with no replies was making me feel more and more depressed. I had no way to even call them at home because the last time I was there they didn't have a phone. I had the snooker to look forward to in March, and it had been over a year since the results of the DNA and no news from Angola. That long I had waited for a response and indeed I had a choice to do something about it.

On January 17, 2001, I published a story on *Daily News*, claiming for the body of my father to be exhumed. Surely with that article I would receive response from the family and waited for weeks, until one day, a call came through my mobile phone and it was the Bulgarian ambassador Mr. Valentin Kazakov. He wouldn't tell me over the phone the reason for the invitation to the embassy the following week, but I just presumed it had something to do with my documents. Victor and I went together, and we were accepted by Mrs. Katia Deleva who at the time was the consul. We all entered the office of the ambassador and were invited to sit. I was still very anxious to know what it was all about and was waiting to be told. The ambassador raised himself from his chair and stood behind it. He was furious and could hardly hide it. He then told me that he had received a phone call from the widow of my father. She asked the ambassador to do anything in his power to stop me writing nonsense about her late husband and that she has been unable to sleep ever since I appeared with my claims. The ambassador said that Mrs. Maria told him that the DNA test results were negative and a copy had been sent to me for clarification and that I should stop once and for all with this or else I wouldn't "see another daylight." All this was said in front of the Bulgarian consul and my husband. I couldn't believe what I was hearing! He was there to protect me as a Bulgarian citizen, not threaten me. Victor and I left the office fuming, and Victor himself was speechless. He convinced me not to do anything for his sake, let things cool, but I wouldn't let things go.

My new snooker season began from where I left it. I won thirty-three games again out of thirty-six, and the league was won by my team and then I went on to win the singles for the C division league. Then I defended my ladies' singles for the 2001 and won the Mashonaland Handy Cup Singles. Another successful year in terms of achievements in snooker, and again I dedicated my trophies to the club. In each of my singles finals, Victor wasn't there and that just couldn't be forgiven. I was happy by January because I received an invitation from the World Ladies' Snooker Association to play in April at the world championship, and the news was just so inspiring for me. I could be playing for my country Bulgaria on the big stage in the world, which was in England. Also in four years' time I could go and visit my home city of Pliska and my daughter. I was missing her hugely, and all this was such an opportunity.

I was practicing with even more desire than before. I wanted to prove a point or something to all these people who had rejected me from their lives that I was a capable person and, with the little opportunities I had in life, could still make it! But things were never as easy for me as for some others. Victor came to me one night with the news that he was going to England too. At first I thought that he wanted to be there with me to watch me play snooker, but it was for totally different reasons. He told me that his mother wished him to travel to the UK and try to get a job, which could help the business that was going under. They had literally lost money on the pub and the house could be taken from them as well if somebody didn't do something about it, and that someone was Victor. Of course, he didn't let me into details when he intend to travel and where he was going to stay in the UK, and in a week's time he was gone. I didn't even get invited to the airport to see him off. He just hugged me at the house and said that he'd be waiting for me in the UK, and his family would be looking after me so as to make sure I was okay and he left.

I was looking through the window wondering if I was going to see him soon. I only had two months before going to the World Ladies' Championship, but those two months would be the longest ever in terms of being alone in a country where the closest people I had were my snooker teammates. Victor's family promised him to invite me for the weekends and make sure I didn't get too lonely and be around their company. Of course, the reality was different. I was phoning after three or four days to his mother to hear of any news from Victor and she would only say that he was okay and she had spoken to him, but he'd left no message for me. I had no phone contact for Victor in the UK and was only hoping that he'd call me. For weeks I waited for his call, but nothing. I knew he was going to definitely call me on my birthday. I was at the club practicing snooker on the twenty-sixth of February, my birthday. With my mobile phone next to me, I was waiting for the call from Victor, at the same time waiting for my teammates to arrive anytime for the team picture with the trophies.

Then the door to the room I was in opened, and it was Mr. Madondo, the person that was working at the bar who would often come and let us know if someone had called. This time he looked very sad and had tears in his eyes. He just couldn't tell me what it was, and I had to ask him. It was Francis. He'd been found dead in front of his house, attacked by armed men and beaten savagely. He couldn't make it to the hospital and had died.

I was devastated and couldn't pick myself up for days and stayed locked in my room. Francis's wife was expecting a baby, and I later I learned that on the night he was killed she had delivered a baby boy whom she named after his father. I was devastated, and all I was thinking was where was Victor for me when I needed him? He phoned me later that night to wish me happy birthday, but it wasn't happy. His family hadn't contacted me in weeks and didn't bother to check if I was still alive, especially knowing that Victor must have told them that I had lost a good friend and the captain of my team. Weeks after the funeral, I revisited the snooker club and tried to restore focus on the task ahead of me, but found it very hard and tiring. I hadn't eaten healthy food for weeks and had lost a massive amount of weight, which was affecting my physical strength. Before, I had been able to go on for four or five hours without getting tired of practicing. I had a month to go to the world championship and Victor was in England trying to find a job. One of his uncles lived near London and worked as a lawyer, and he was going to help him find a job for a short while and perhaps lend him some money, which I was going to use to travel to the UK.

On another hand, life in Zuland was becoming impossible for living. The poverty was hitting the country hard, and it was getting difficult even to find bread and milk in the shops. Sometimes I'd get up very early and in fact had to queue to buy bread, which had to last me for days. Not many shops managed to see their supplies delivered because somewhere halfway, the road-organized thieves would steal it and distribute it among the opposition fighters. So in a way, what they stole they had stolen from the government and in return the government would send the war veterans who would sometimes attack innocent people. For the same reasons, I stopped working in the hairdresser salon.

One day I was scared if I was going to make it out alive. We were about to leave work when a fight occurred outside the building between the government troops and some civilians. Some of the civilians ran into the salon where myself and other four women were ready to leave, only to be held inside because one of the guys held the door that he eventually locked. He thought he'd get away with it, but for the most idiotic thing, the police fired a tear gas through the window that spread so fast; it was something I have only seen on TV. I couldn't breathe and quickly covered my mouth with a towel that I managed to grab from one of the nearby tables. I had completely lost recollection of where I was when I found myself pushed outside the building and forced to lie on the ground with everyone else. I could hardly believe what was happening because I wasn't involved in anything that I know and surely I shouldn't be there. We were checked and eventually released, but that shock I have witnessed was enough for me to realize that my place wasn't in that country. This wasn't my fight and surely I wasn't going to be dragged into it and stopped from going to work, and what a relief it was! For days the streets would be ruled by riots, but the police could do very little as shops and people's houses were burned. At point, I was worried about Victor's parents because they lived on a farm in a place that was isolated, so they were more vulnerable than the others. The only way to ensure that they were okay was through Victor when he phoned me because I was scared to go on my own across town and take on a minibus to the farm. I'd also heard that some of the country roads had been closed by the government troops to prevent opposition fighters from getting into the city. For some days I didn't practice snooker because the club wouldn't be open for fear of the riots.

I was hours away from traveling to the UK with my luggage and ticket all in one place sorted out. Now all I had to do was wait for Eleanor to arrive. She'd promised to drive me to the airport and was supposed to be there within half an hour. I was waiting and just hoping that everything would go according to plan, when my mobile phone rang, and it was her. She apologized that she couldn't make it and that she would book a taxi for me and wished me a safe trip. That was the last I heard from her before I left Zuland. The taxi did get to me on time and had to drive fast to make up for the lost time as the road to the airport was closed and only people with tickets were allowed to pass through (some measures taken by the government to prevent the rioters from attacking the airport). I checked in and sat on one of the benches with a full view of the electronic screen. I was thinking about the life I was leaving behind and whether I should come and live in this country again. Victor never discussed his plans for the future and indeed how I featured in those plans. I know we'd have a lot of catching up to do when we meet in the UK the next day. I certainly was allowed to stay in the country for three months but no more than that. Victor was either going to have to come with me to Bulgaria or stay behind in the UK, but whatever he needed to understand that I was his wife and should be his priority.

On the plane, I could hardly sleep. My thoughts were engaged in some few good moments I had in Zuland, such as winning snooker tournaments, and then the sad loss of my friend, Francis. Without him, I wouldn't be on the plane to the UK to play snooker in the world championship, representing my country of birth. What pride I felt just thinking about it, knowing that I was about to write my name in the history of Bulgarian snooker as the first player to represent it, hoping that my mother and my daughter and maybe one day my father's family would recognize my achievement. But the question was, was I ready? Mentally I'd been weakened by the events that had happened in my recent life, and the focus wasn't there. I knew it would be crucial for me to regain some of my energy in the next few days.

I arrived at Heathrow Airport a week before the championship and passed through all the passport checks, being allowed to enter the country on my snooker visa. Victor was waiting for me at the exit as he'd promised and helped me with the luggage. He was excited to see me and yet had that expression of a person who knew he had done the wrong thing by leaving me behind in a country that was becoming the most dangerous place to be. We got to the car that Victor had borrowed from his uncle and drove to his house in Feltham. It was a small house with two bedrooms on the second floor and a bath. The kitchen was located on the ground floor with the lounge next to it. Most of the time his uncle would be at work, and Victor and I would have the house to ourselves.

In one of those days when we were alone, Victor sat me down to explain why he'd done everything in a quiet way and kept away from me. He said it was his mother's idea (like I needed to guess that!) and that his situation was not as simple as I might think. He told me that he was refused entrance to the country when he arrived, and the only way to stay was to do what his mother asked him, which was to become an asylum seeker and use the current situation in the country as his reason. I wasn't sure what all that meant and how it affected me until he explained further. In order for me to stay with him as his wife in the UK, I had to join him and that also meant that I had to give up the Bulgarian citizenship because otherwise I wouldn't qualify since Bulgaria wasn't in a civil war. Then I suggested to him about us moving to Bulgaria to start there; the chances of him finding a job were very good, and he spoke the language. We went all day arguing about it, and he wouldn't give in. It wasn't that simple because his mother was involved. She also wanted to move to the UK, and she needed his help to achieve this. I'd been so stupid and should have seen it coming, but didn't. Victor took me some days later to Swindon, the venue of the World Ladies' Championship and we didn't talk for the most part of the journey. I was really cross with him for not seeing that our marriage was falling apart and he wanted me to become part of something that I wouldn't accept as asylum seeker in the UK, whereas we could be free and start fresh in America even, where there were so many opportunities for him as an engineer and me to play pool.

I'd already left my daughter and my life behind to be with him in Zuland, but he still wanted more of me and which was to give away my citizenship of birth.

I had to think all this through before I made my decision to tell Victor what I thought of his idea (or his mother's to be more accurate). At the championship, I was nervous and didn't play up to my standard level, which could have taken me through the group stages, and so I lost in my first match of the group against the eventual champion Kelly Fisher in straight games. For Kelly, it was business as usual on the table, and for me it was the humiliation of not producing when it mattered in the match. I had my chances and couldn't execute them.

The following day was pretty much the same story. I lost to Natasha Nierman in straight games and then to Wendy Jans and was dropped to play in the plate competition, where I managed to reach the semifinal but lost in best of three games to a girl representing Holland. To be honest, I was disappointed that I didn't do better than I'd expected to do, but I promised I was going to come back stronger next year. I got in touch with the organizers of the event and Mrs. Mandy Fisher, a former world champion in women snooker and chairman of the WBSA. We spoke of the possibility of me joining the women ranking events that year 2002 and of the importance that would play in the improvement of my game. I certainly wanted to do it and, if possible, become something like a semiprofessional player. I could see my future back then with snooker, but couldn't say the same about my marriage to Victor.

After I got back to London, we spent time together trying to figure out what we were going to do. Still Victor tried to pursue me not to leave for Bulgaria but stay with him as a wife supporting her husband in his battle. I was trapped in a very difficult situation. I hadn't seen my daughter for four long years and missed her a lot, and despite knowing that it was going to be very hard for me to find a place to stay, I decided this was the right decision for me. Victor wasn't happy at all, but that was the right decision because his uncle wanted him to leave his house and I didn't want to be another obstacle for him.

I arrived back home in Bulgaria after a long time abroad with no place to stay. I had kept a notebook with some contact numbers of friends that I could always rely on and phone at any time, but I chose not to call them but find a place for a few nights and then look for something else more permanent. I was excited and nervous at the same time to be back home. I was scared of meeting my daughter who was now ten years old and who could easily reject me as her mother. I had no idea how she'd been brought up for the past years and wasn't sure if I was making the right choice to get back into her life. All sorts of thoughts crossed my mind that first night in the hotel room. I was not very far from where my daughter was. In the morning, I was going to wait patiently in a coffee shop that was positioned perfectly for me to see who was coming in and out of their building. I spent my whole morning there without seeing anyone that I knew from Ivan's family. I was worried that perhaps they didn't live there anymore and that nobody had cared to inform me about it. So I stretched my legs and started walking toward the apartment. I could see that some people were staring at me with curiosity, wondering who I was and particularly what I was doing in their neighborhood. I didn't know how much Bulgaria had changed since I left, but I was certain that I had changed and I no longer cared about the attitude of others. I had to find my daughter and that was the only reason I came back to Bulgaria, but if I had been aware of the people around, I would have avoided the kick in the stomach that came from my left side! I found myself on the ground and stayed there covering my head to protect from the next kick. I heard lots of noise coming from the near apartment as somebody tried to scare my attackers with the threat of police, so they did run away but not before I was struck a few more times. I was on the ground until I heard someone saying that it was fine to get up and walk away. I was scared that this incident could have been seen by my daughter if she was still in her apartment, which was something I needed to find out. I ignored all the "trying to help me" people around, "a little too late" for some who did nothing, and walked inside the building. I climbed the stairs quickly and found a different name at the door that used to be Ivan's family name on it. I hesitated for a little while and then pushed the button. No sign of anyone at home, and just when I was about to take the elevator, a neighbor's door opened and it was someone that I vaguely remembered seeing before. He obviously knew what I was coming for and gave me guidance to the new address of my daughter. So they had moved to the house, of course, where I had spent time with Ivan when I had no other place to go.

I headed there with my heart racing inside me and emotional feelings fighting to come out. I reached the gate and looked around to find a doorbell or any other way of signaling my presence when a dog did the job for me. The dog was big and looked frightening, so I stayed in my position and waited for someone to show up under the continuous barking. Luiza's grandfather came out, and I didn't need any introductions for him to invite me in. Luiza wasn't there, and her father was at work too. I was offered a drink and a plate with biscuits. Then Ivan's dad joined me and asked me about my intentions. I didn't know how long we talked when I heard the voice of a girl playing outside with the dog. She was coming home from a swimming lesson, and there was a surprise waiting for her in the kitchen. Her grandmother was the first to see me, and from her reaction, it was obvious that I wasn't welcomed in the house. Luiza followed her into the kitchen, and she was the most beautiful girl that I have ever seen! She knew who I was and ran straight into my open arms to the surprise and shock of her grandmother. We held each other, and her grandparents could do nothing else but leave us alone.

Obviously, we both missed each other hugely, yet in a strange way we were also strangers. I could understand from where Ivan's mother was coming from. She would have expected me to phone and arrange a time and date to visit my daughter, but I didn't know if they had a phone for contact; also, if they had read my letters that I had sent, they surely would know that I was coming to Bulgaria. However, none of this mattered anymore to me because I had my daughter in my arms and nothing and no one would be able to prevent our bond. We talked and I learned from my daughter that it was her auntie who was collecting all my letters and kept them for Luiza, and my daughter kept all my photos under her pillow hidden from her father. I had dedicated my first trophy from the World Ladies' Championship to her, and she took it from me with pride and I promised her that there will be many more to come one day. We connected for hours until her father arrived from work and with mixed emotions greeted me. It was hard to tell if he missed me at all, but I was invited out for a drink and more like for a one-on-one conversation. I was expecting him to tell me things of the sort that I shouldn't have come and that Luiza was fine and has accepted that I am not in her life and they don't need me to be around, that kind of thing; but instead I ended up sitting opposite a man at a cafe table who was crying and telling me how hard it had been for him to let me go all those years and that he'd never stopped loving me. I was totally confused and was trying to think how best to deal with all he'd said without having to make things complicated with my daughter. I had to remind Ivan that I was married and loved my husband very much and would never in a million years get involved with someone else even if it was the father of my child. I knew that it all very much depended on Ivan how often I could see my daughter now. Of course, I still didn't have a permanent place to stay in Pliska because nothing at that stage was decided. My husband was in the UK trying to get permission to stay and work through a lawyer, and if things did go his way, I was going to follow him there.

In any case, I didn't have much to offer my daughter but to visit more often than before. Whether Ivan was secretly hoping to have a second chance with me or not, he allowed me to visit my daughter every weekend and not only that, but after I'd settled and found a place to stay, he would bring her over to my place and we'd all go out like families do. Yet in my mind I knew where I belonged and he needed to accept that he'd never have another chance with me. The only problem I saw was that wherever we went with my daughter he had to be there too, and partly that was down to Luiza. She loved her father and wanted him to be with us without realizing that we were not together. I'd be lying if I said that I didn't enjoy the time being together as a "family," thinking how things could've been different only if he'd been strong enough then to marry me and if maybe I wasn't colored, which was the real factor. His parents were less influential now maybe due to the fact that they were getting older and less demanding since Ivan too was getting older and needed to find a wife.

On the days when I wasn't with my daughter, I had all the motivation to practice hard at snooker and looked forward to the beginning of the new snooker season in England. I also used the spare time to find out what the outcome of the investigation was against my sister. The result was that no facts had been found to suggest any crime against her and so my claim was dismissed. Of course, I was given a time frame to appeal that, but since I wasn't around, the investigation was dismissed. I could have hired a lawyer if I had more money to get deep into her disappearance all those years ago, but that would have meant my mother being questioned and the involvement of many other people. I believed that everything was leading in one direction, and that was home, the country of my father. That was the reason why my sister was missing. My mother and her friend used her all those years ago pretending she was me while my father was sending money to her.

I also went to the Bulgarian newspaper *Noshten Trud* to publicize my story from Zuland and how I was treated by the Bulgarian ambassador in Zuland, which was followed by his resignation in the same year, which I can assume had something to do with my complaint. I also tried to get an apartment from the services, which I could start paying for and eventually buy, but I would have to wait for years as the list of registered people was huge. From what I knew, people like me had the priority to receive an apartment from the state before others with living family members, yet I was still behind many who had some properties to their name. There was nothing for me to do, but just hope that I would qualify one day and would have the opportunity to have my daughter living with me.

In the meantime, I decided to contact the Bulgarian billiard association and register as a snooker player, hoping to receive some sponsorship, but that didn't work out. The problem was that there wasn't a snooker association in the country at the time, and I had to try to find my own sponsorship for the coming snooker season in England. I even used one of the papers in Bulgaria *7Days Sport* to publish an article about my achievements in Zuland as well with my participation in the World Ladies' Championship in Swindon that same year in 2002. That didn't help either, and I was left with practicing and hoping to find a different way of supporting myself. Victor was out of the equation for helping me financially as he wasn't working himself and relied on his uncle. Also from what I learned around that time, he'd found a place in Slough. The trouble with that was he was in a house with around five men from different nationalities from Africa, and they were all just like him, asylum seekers. That, of course, kept bringing the police to the house for formal checks. Many of the people who had been refused asylum had to go back to their countries, but many didn't do it immediately as they had jobs and were sending money to their families back home. So the police would do the job of ensuring that nobody stayed in the country after refusal.

I had things to worry about Victor, especially because he had all to lose. It was too late for him to come to Bulgaria because his passport was held by the Home Office, and his case was waiting to be heard in front of a commission. He had a lawyer to represent him, and that same lawyer told him that his case would be very hard to represent because he was married to a Bulgarian woman, who presented him with the choice to live in Bulgaria. That unfortunately was not how Victor and his mother saw the situation. He felt he needed to find a way to stay in the UK and not give up on me at the same time. I had found myself a job from nine to five and was happy with the money I was earning, and they could help me travel to the UK. The job was in a factory, and my involvement was to pack curtain poles in a box and seal it. The job was pretty boring because no skills were required, but was convenient with the area I lived in and no transport was needed. My salary was paid in cash every Friday and helped me to never be short of money, and most of the times after work, I got involved in playing pool for money, which doubled my earnings.

That is how my life was for the time being until I was ready to travel to the UK for the beginning of August 2002. I was given a six-months visa to play snooker after I had paid for all the tournaments in advance and received the letter of invitation by the World Ladies' Snooker Association. I was on the top of the world of excitement! I had a dream, and I wanted to see it come true. I said my goodbyes with Luiza and promised to stay in touch with her by phone every week. Of course, having my daughter back in my life gave me that extra energy and ambition for achieving my goal, and I felt that whatever I was doing wasn't just for me anymore. She was the meaning in everything I did when it came to life decisions.

I was in the UK reunited with Victor and happy to be with him after almost five months of separation. There wasn't any change to his situation because his lawyer wanted him to provide more evidence for his case and the people who wanted to help him from Zuland were not doing things the way Victor wanted. I was staying in his place, which was only one small room on the ground floor next to the front door that often banged loud when someone came in or went out. That, of course, affected our sleep, but Victor would rather have that then enter into a fight with some of the guys who really looked dangerous to me. I avoided being in the kitchen at the same time with any of them while they were cooking or even standing there talking. Not many of them even knew that I was living in the house. Victor didn't trust them enough to leave me on my own in the room. I got on with my tournaments, not that I was winning, but it did help me develop my game. I also made a friendship with a woman called Sharon who played a part in getting one of her very close friends John to teach me the standard way of playing the game. John was well known among the women snooker circuit for coaching and helping Kim Shaw become a top player and move later to America to play professional pool. I would be practicing with John like three times a week in High Wycombe, and the ultimate prize John was aiming for was the world championship. He always told me of the potential I had and my strong points in the game that were crucial for any player.

We worked hard for months and months on my cue action and break. Building that would ensure I could win a game in one or two visits to the table. Victor obviously wasn't approving that I spent so much time playing snooker, but on the other hand, he knew that this was my life and I had to give it a go. John coached me for free, and the table I played for hours was arranged for free since he was one of the coaches and had the right to play for free there. Sharon and I became very close during that time, and she would be there almost all times when I was practicing and after that would ensure that I returned home safely. The tournaments were spread monthly at different locations in the country, where it was almost impossible for me to attend, so John would ask Sharon to join the event to be there with me for support. I always lacked self-esteem when it came to issues of background and origin; I couldn't help but feel different among all the white English women, and it did reflect more or less in my game. I would play nervously; losing my games was seemingly psychological, and that was something that only time could fix. John couldn't do anything about it, but he still believed in my potential. I didn't win any first prize that season but lost to the finalist in Belgium 147 in the plates in December 2002.

I had a month before my visa expiration, and yet Victor's case wasn't going anywhere. He again wanted me to stay in England and join him as his wife in the seeking for asylum. I categorically refused and said to him that life was already hard enough being Bulgarian as I didn't get any support from social services for accommodation, and the Bulgarian sports federation was not supporting me. He wanted me to forget about snooker and hoped we get permission to stay and live in the UK as long as his country had problems and perhaps return there one day. I didn't see his logic until he brightened things for me and suggested that we should have a baby and if I gave birth in the country then they couldn't send us away. That idea just totally put me off everything; I liked this man, but he'd lost my respect. He was ready to use all sorts of ways to stay in this country, and that included me.

I returned to Bulgaria in 2003 and resumed my work and practice with one eye on the championship in April. I was looking for sponsorship again and without any luck again, and the people I thought could help me had all become distanced from me. I advertised in newspapers and had to pay for it, and that didn't help. It was ironic that I was playing for Bulgaria and representing the country in the prestigious tournament, and nobody was willing to invest in me. Everything I did was the hard way and by myself. I had spoken with Victor a couple of times over the phone and learned from him that he had a job somewhere, but wouldn't tell me where and how he got the job. He somehow managed to arrange for his mother to come to the UK, and even she had a date for a job interview. That was the good news he shared with me, and he couldn't wait to see me soon. I had paid my fee for participation in the World Ladies' and received the invitation with which I went to the UK embassy in Pliska somewhere in March 2003. On paper, everything looked solid for me to receive the visa for the World Ladies' Championship, but that wasn't the case. The consul at the embassy refused to grant me a visa based on the grounds that if I was going only for the World Ladies' Championship, then the visa that was given to me can't be anything but six months. So therefore what I was going to do during the remaining five months after the tournament was the question. I didn't intend to stay beyond the championship and made it clear at the interview, but that obviously didn't count. They asked me where my husband was at the time, and I told the truth that he was in the UK looking for asylum. I pointed out that that wasn't my intention since I was Bulgarian and had no reason to do the same. I pointed out that if I'd wanted, I would have done it a long time ago too and explained that each time I had been in the country I had always stayed within the limited time and never overstayed. The next question was if I had relatives in Bulgaria, and I responded in the negative. Obviously that gave them food for thought that since I didn't have family in Bulgaria, I might find no reason to be back although I mentioned that my daughter lived in Bulgaria and I have no intentions to be abroad. I waited for hours before I was called into a small room with a window that separated me from the person who gave me the bad news.

I was in tears and couldn't help crying. He left the room and I was still sitting there in agony that everything I was working for and the hours of practicing snooker to play in the biggest event of any snooker player was refused to me, based on the suspicion that I might consider emigrating to the UK and that I'd failed to show evidence that I would be returning to Bulgaria. The news, of course, came as a shock to many people in the UK involved with the women's snooker. I had also been given ten days to appeal for the decision and had to pay another significant amount of money for someone to look at my case on top of the amount, which was huge by Bulgarian standards, I had to pay for the visa application. Of course, I didn't get to go to the World Ladies' in the UK and focused on my work and practicing snooker, which had to help me accept the disappointment. Victor had a choice to withdraw his asylum application and move with me to Bulgaria, but he chose not to. We were going to be separated for a whole year, and there was nothing I could have done to be with him. We stayed in touch through phone calls twice a week, which was later reduced to once a week. Our main communication became e-mail, and of course, he felt obligated to send me money whenever he could, just to make sure that I wasn't short. We both had to stay strong for each other and our marriage. I had to believe that things would get better one day, but it was hard. One thing was my snooker career, jeopardized by not having played for months, and the other was my marriage, a whole year's separation. If anything else, England was the last place I wanted to go again, but the problem was that Victor was there and he wouldn't move from there. He had his mother moving to the country and was collecting reasons to stay.

In the meantime, I spent more time with my daughter and got involved as an extra in movies such as the *Mosquito Man* and a few others. I continued playing snooker to get my mind off everything. On the other hand, a conversation with my daughter about my family in Africa brought up the long painful process I had to go through with the DNA test and how I had tried communicate since. She had the right to know about everything in my life and details such as who her grandfather was and where his family come from, something I wanted her to be proud of. She'd listen to my stories and always ask if anything would happen one day with my recognition. She would never understand that it was not that simple to be recognized as anyone's daughter if they were a president and had passed away.

I know that more than anything I wanted to continue fighting to prove that the late president was my father because I'd started it already and if I would be achieving a result for the hundreds and thousands of children like me who'd been left around the world, denied of their identity.

I owed that to my daughter and the children of her children. My mother already had stolen my right to have a family by giving me up for adoption, but my father never did and in fact was a man of great principle. So my battle to be recognized by the family never stopped, and in fact I had made my decision. I was going to face them, and I was going to travel to them, my family in Africa. I didn't know when, but I knew it was going to be soon. The danger was that nothing would happen and I possibly would end up dead and buried somewhere never to be found, but that was the price I was willing to pay by confronting them once and for all alone. I was threatened once before by the Bulgarian ambassador in Zuland and then later told by the deputy foreign minister that my life was in danger and some people wanted me dead. Well, if that was true, then I wasn't afraid of dying for the right cause as opposed to being denied my identity. I knew that the ticket to my father's country would cost a fortune, and I had started saving money from work and from the money Victor was sending me to make that happen. I never mentioned to my daughter the potential of something happening to me in Africa and the nature of the importance that it was for the family of my father not to recognize me, and at any cost they could stop me if they wanted to.

At the same time in 2003, the snooker world was shocked by the decision made by the British government to ban tobacco from sponsoring sports events. Of course, that had an immediate effect on the game by forcing out many of the top snooker women players and following the footsteps of Allison Fisher in America.

The women snooker received no funds from the embassy, which meant that they had to rely on themselves and small businesses run by family and friends for support, but it was not enough to keep its top players. For many women, playing snooker had no meaning, which was pretty much the case for me. I was considering a move to America, where I could follow my dream of playing pool, but not before I went to see my family in Africa.

I had no need to tell Victor how hard it was going to be for me to visit the UK just to play snooker in tournaments that wouldn't cover half of my spending. I wanted us to move together somewhere where we both had the opportunity to do what we love, but he wasn't with me and his dreams were no longer mine. The marriage was coming to an end, yet neither one of us was able to say it to the other. We were trapped together, and Victor needed me more than I did. I was ready to move on with my life, but he didn't know. I couldn't tell him that; I'd made a pledge when we married to stay by him even if it was deconstructed by distance. He made it easy for me one day, however, by admitting to having a relationship with a woman from his workplace though it that wasn't serious. I wasn't convinced about them not seeing each other, but I really didn't care anymore. I was going to come to the UK for the next World Snooker Championship and I was going to put our marriage to an end.

In April 2004, I was allowed to play snooker in the World Ladies', but I didn't go. I also lost my snooker coach John, who suffered a major injury after he had been attacked by men and died in February the same year from his injuries. I had to tell Victor that our marriage was over, and the easy way to do that was to tell him I had met someone and wanted a divorce. Victor wasn't having it and said that he would fight for me and our marriage that hadn't been consummated for a year. I stayed with him for some months to try to resolve our marriage, but the damage was done long before, and his mother being in the equation didn't help either. He was spending his weekends going to her house, helping her with everything she wanted, which was just too much to take. She was always going to be his first in his choice and I second. It was a sad period for him to digest that it was all over and I need to move on with my life. While I was in the UK, I attempted to get a visa to visit my father's country, but without any luck. I had a few meetings at the time with Mr. Monis, who worked at the embassy in London and dealt with my problem. I requested that he put me in touch with the deputy foreign minister, who was the person involved in Zuland, and he promised to pass my message to him. I waited for any news from the family and kept phoning at the embassy when one day I was told that the deputy foreign minister had been found dead that same year. I didn't know what to think of that news at the time, but he was the one dealing with my case and now was gone!

I left the UK in September 2004 and went back to Bulgaria just for a few months, which made my separation with my daughter brief and less painful. I didn't want to get emotional again and had to believe that things would be okay. I left for Germany in October, only after my visit to Bulgaria. I was going to stay with Nina, whom I believed was my sister Daniela. She couldn't have me in her apartment because her mother stayed with her at the time, and of course, we wanted to keep my visit to Germany as quiet as possible. Nina was going to help me get a visa from the embassy in Berlin, and it all had to be done very quietly. Nobody at the embassy had to suspect who I was and my real intentions of visiting the country. Nina also knew what she was getting into by helping me get in my father's country. She understood the importance of my desire for going there and that I was left with no other choice. She tried to change my mind by encouraging me to think of my daughter, but I was indeed thinking of my daughter!

I spent the next few months wandering the streets of Berlin, waiting for the time when my sister had to travel for one of her trips to the capital Luanda, which was going to be in November. She had a relative with whom I was going to be safe, and he was going to look after me for a month, which was the maximum visa I was going to obtain. Nina was going to help me with the application form and the reason for my visit, which was to visit a relative. The fact that I didn't speak Portuguese could have been something they'd pick up on, as Nina's intention was to travel for only one week and then return to Germany though I intended to stay for a whole month. What I was relying on was that they had never heard about me through other embassies' representatives because that would be a problem. On the other hand, that was possible, as the woman who had replaced the late deputy foreign minister was no other than my half sister Dr. Irene.

So the time arrived when both Nina and I were ready with the paperwork and waiting at the embassy foyer. We were both nervous, me that nothing goes wrong with my application and I get the visa on that same day and Nina that she wouldn't get caught for lying that she was my sister on paper. We had hours to wait before being asked to go into the office of the consul. Obviously, all this was standard routine questioning of the candidates for visa, but Nina was nervous because she wasn't expecting to be called with me. Well, the worst-case scenario I was imagining was that somebody made a check on me and had contacted the foreign ministry for any previous records of my visiting the country and they'd discover who I was through my name. Anyway, that was only my thought at the time, and as we got inside the office, we were asked to answer a few questions such as how we were related. For some reason, they had to ask that question because when Nina received her nationality, she was asked to list family members, and as I wasn't on that list, it needed explaining. Nina stayed calm and just answered that as I'd been left in the orphanage we'd only been reunited a few years back. The consul was making his decision quietly, and I had the feeling for a second that there was more he wanted to ask, but he didn't. He finished with us and asked us to wait in the foyer again, which meant hours, and when we saw everyone leaving, even the staff, I got worried. Something wasn't right, and we shouldn't be still sitting for hours not knowing what was happening. My sister was getting impatient, and whenever she saw a member of the staff that she knew, she wanted to know what was happening behind those doors. None of the staff would give any information to citizens because it's simply crucial to their job, but it made my sister feel better by knowing that at least she was trying. Finally, our waiting came to an end when the secretary of the consul came out of the office holding my passport. He passed me my passport and said thank you. I returned the words to him and looked inside the passport while the secretary was walking back to his office. Nina was just as much excited as me to find out if I'd been a successful candidate and I was!

I couldn't express that feeling; to know I had the ticket and passport ready to travel to Africa, the country of my father and his predecessors. I was once in Africa, but this time was different. The place I was about to go had meaning to my existence and everything about me. That was the place I belonged, and the closer I was getting to travel there, the more I knew I was destined to be part of that country. I had never felt so drawn to a country before and yet haven't been there. I'd been ready for this trip forever, and no danger could prevent my going there. For me, this was a historical moment, and I had to capture every moment of it. I prepared in my bag only summer clothes and took my camera with me. Nina had already left for Africa; maybe I was going to see her there or maybe not. She told me that her schedule in the capital was very tight, and she would have to stay close to the people meeting. She was staying in a hotel that was farther away from where I was going to stay, and that was going to make it hard for her to come and see me.

My flight wasn't direct and required one night's sleep over in Brussels and so from Berlin on November 6, 2004. I flew to the capital of Belgium where I spent the night at the airport, and the following morning on the seventh, I was on my flight to my fatherland. The flight was going to be very long, and we were expected there in the evening. I had a long peaceful sleep on the plane and nothing to worry about. I knew Nina's cousin would wait there for me and I had his mobile phone number written in my notebook, and as Nina was in Luanda, I had nothing to worry about.

Angola

My flight was pleasant, and the next stage was passport checking. I was impressed with the way the line of people moved fast, and I also went through the passport checking without problems. Now all I had to do was wait in the arrival area to be noticed by Nina's cousin Alcides, who should have the details of how I look. I had no coins to make a call to my sister to let her know I had arrived safe and sound in the country. So I sat and waited a long time without any signs of Alcides. Minutes turned into almost an hour when I was approached by a man who asked me if I needed any help. He spoke good English, and just like me, he was waiting to be given a lift by his girlfriend. We got into conversation, and I learned that he was an international student and was traveling back home for the holidays and in particular for the Independence Day that same month. Time was passing during our conversation, and there was still no sign of Alcides. I began to worry because it wasn't something I would have expected from Nina's cousin. My worries continued after I got in the car with the man I had only met at the airport. His girlfriend was kind to offer to take me to the house where Alcides lived. I was uncertain if I'd done the right thing to get into a car with a complete stranger, but there wasn't a better choice, and they didn't look like suspicious.

The capital was lively in the evening and very warm that I was pleased not to be wearing too many clothes. The journey didn't last long when the car pulled up in front of a big house. Obviously, whoever lived in the house was rich or he wouldn't have gone to the trouble of having a speaker outside the automatic gate. I got out of the car and pressed the button, and before I even said anything, the gate slid open and a young man stood in front of me. He must have seen the lights of the car and decided to come and see for himself.

I greeted him in English because that was the only international language that I knew and asked him if this was the house where Alcides lived. The young man's facial expression changed as he only now realized who I was and that he should have been picking me up from the airport. He looked shocked that I was a day earlier and wasn't expecting me until tomorrow! Well, knowing my sister and the number of things she had to deal with before leaving Germany, I wasn't surprised that she'd given him the wrong date. The couple that gave me a lift had to apologize because they were also in a hurry to be somewhere else but were glad to see me safely delivered. I thanked them and watched them drive away before I followed Alcides inside the house.

There was a young girl relaxing with a drink in front of her while listening to music, and as soon as she saw me, she rose and walked to the CD player to stop the music. Alcides introduced us, and she, just like him, was surprised to see me a day earlier. I felt uncomfortable, knowing that these two young people were in the middle of something and there was me a day early. Great! It was very late to make any attempt to try calling Nina, so I decided to do it first thing in the morning. I was taken to the guest room and offered something to eat if I was hungry, but I refused politely. All I needed was to rest and wished "sleep well" to both of them. I couldn't sleep that first night realizing that I was finally in the country of my father and how exciting it would be to meet with the family. My original plan of contacting them was through the deputy foreign minister, but he wasn't around anymore. The next person I could contact and let know I was here was the sister of my late father and my aunt Mrs. Ruth. I had to find her number, and for that reason, I needed Nina's help. Nina could help me exchange currency and find a basic secondhand mobile phone to use for contacts in the country. She could also help me learn the easy way to travel from the house to town and tell me which areas were safe to walk and which to avoid. I needed to maximize my limited time in the country of my father's birth. A whole month, I thought, was plenty of time to meet with the family and find a solution to the problem that involved us from the DNA test that was "inconclusive," and my aim was to have another test.

The next day was hot and sunny. I got a knock on the door that the breakfast had been served and if I wished to join them. I didn't hesitate and wanted to start my first day in Luanda with a promise of success. I had my usual tea and cheese on toast while Alcides and his girlfriend had cereal, which was one thing I never got used to eating when I lived in Zuland. We talked while eating and I was offered to join them for a day out to the beach, but that wasn't on my mind. They didn't know why I was in the country in the first place and presumed that I was only there on holiday to relax. I came up with the excuse that Nina would visit me that day and the two of us would go out to town so that they wouldn't feel obligated to spend their time with me but go ahead with their own arrangements. Eventually when I was on my own, I had to think of another way of getting in touch with my aunt Ruth. So I found the telephone book under the phone desk and started searching for my aunt's name, hoping she'd be among the others. There were many with her name, which I had to note, hoping that one would be her. She was the first person I would contact to inform that I was in the country. From her reaction when I last saw her in Zuland, I knew that she wasn't expecting what she saw in me. My resemblance with my father was something that shocked her, and she had to run almost immediately when we were introduced in another room. This time I was in their home yard and for her sake she had no place to run, and sooner or later she had to face me again, or at least that was what I was hoping to happen. I dialed the first number on the list, and the phone rang and rang with nobody to answer so I moved on to the next. It wasn't long before someone answered this line. It was a woman who couldn't understand me, and I was about to put the handset down when someone took the phone from her and it was her. My aunt was on the other end of the line, and she was surprised to hear my voice and even more surprised to learn that I was in the same country as her. She sounded very tired over the phone and explained to me that she wasn't feeling very well at this moment in time but would love to meet with me. She promised me to contact the family and arrange for us to meet very soon. I told her that my time in the country was limited, which she needed to consider.

I felt great after the conversation with my aunt and had no other reason to believe that the family wouldn't meet with me. For the next few days, I just sat back and enjoyed my stay in the country. Nina did come to see me but not on the day she promised, and when she came to see me, it was to ask me to lend her some money—unbelievable! I needed to save every penny that I could for any unexpected expenses. Anyway, days later, the whole nation was warming up for the biggest party in the country. Streets were busy with children from every age group trying to sell me everything they could for Independence Day, from T-shirts with the image of my father to a flag with the ruling party logo on it. I bought a T-shirt and left the change to the young boy who was ever so delighted. I did intend to wear the image of my father on Independence Day and be there too.

The big day came, and we all were going out to the statue of my father, the place where a speech by the current president would be given in front of thousands of people including international guests. My father's whole family would be there too, but I could only watch them from a distance. I had no intentions to spoil their day although they might have already heard from

Aunt Ruth that I was in the country and precautions were probably taken against me. As always, there were some people who didn't like the current government and came along drunk, singing against the president and his associates but posed no harm. I was with Alcides and his girlfriend who were protecting me from either side. Lots of men were drunk and singing loud while the president was giving his speech, but each time my father's name was mentioned, the audience was cheering up and crying loud his name. I couldn't understand much that was said about my father, but was happy to be there and feel the atmosphere from the side of the citizens. I had tears in my eyes when at the end of the speech I heard the words which had been said by my father in a speech during the liberation of the country: "A luta continua, vitoria e certa." Words that I had to keep holding on to in my fight for recognition against the family of my father for many years.

The president's speech was followed by minutes of silence when flowers were placed in front of my father's statue and then followed by juniors from the ruling party singing before the crowd started to disperse. People were leaving to continue celebrations elsewhere, so we made our way back to the house. Alcides wasn't the kind of person to continue celebrating on the streets, having seen over the years that celebrations could turn into disaster when the people got drunk and got involved in serious conversations that led to subjects like politics. It wasn't easy to talk about life in a country after over twenty years of civil war. The war had ended pretty much with the death of the main opposition leader over two years ago, and there still hadn't been much improvement in the social life of the people. Many blamed the president for the civil war just as much as the dead opposition leader. With the opposition leader, there had been a hope of something new that this country hadn't seen for years since the death of my father, but that hope had died with him hence the frustration of the people was now aimed toward the current president.

For the next days, I was relaxing either alone in the house or going with Alcides and his girlfriend to the seaside for a drink. I was still waiting to hear from Aunt Ruth on the family meeting, as it was already a week of my one-month visit gone and time seemed to be going without any signs of progress.

I phoned my aunt again and asked her if she had arranged the meeting with the family, and she hadn't. I asked to meet with her and even gave her the address where I was staying to come and visit me and she said she would.

I had to find another way of contacting my family about my presence and to force somebody to meet with me. I had no clue what to do, so I went to the national assembly and straight to the office of the Speaker of the parliament.

I waited in his office for almost one hour as his secretary informed him of my presence and the subject of my visit. He didn't wish to see me, and I left his office. I wished to speak with Dr. Irene who also happened to be working for the government at the time.

I was given her number by a person who knew her and phoned to arrange a meeting with her. Dr. Irene wasn't there, and the secretary told me how busy she was and I would have to book an appointment with her. I left my e-mail for communication, and it was not long before I received the e-mail from Dr. Irene with the date and time she would like us to meet.

That was the first time meeting with any of the children of my father. I was happy to meet her in her office that day, but there was so much tension in the air. She knew why I was there, and I didn't know what was on her mind. She offered me a drink as I sat opposite her. She was interested in my past and everything I was doing to that point in my life. Something I found very frustrating over the years is that every person involved with my case wanted to know practically my whole life story but did nothing for me. I just wanted to find a solution to my problem in the country, and I had no time to waste or even much money left for that matter. So I cut to the chase with Dr. Irene and told her why I was in the country. I told her that I needed the DNA test to be redone because I wasn't happy with the "inconclusive" results sent to me years back.

She looked at me, puzzled, and said that she was there in Zuland 1998 when my aunt Ruth came to see me. She told me that they had been sent by the president and that the case was dealt with the government and not the family. Also that the results they had obtained, which had been given to the president, were indeed "negative." I told her she was wrong and that I needed the family to meet and discuss this matter again. The subject was far from over for me and then I left her office.

Days later, I had a very late visitor whom I had never met before who was sent by my aunt Ruth. It was after ten o'clock in the evening, and everyone was in their rooms relaxing when Alcides informed me that someone was in the foyer and would like to meet with me. I quickly put on some proper clothes and, intrigued, went downstairs. Two men were sitting on the sofa, and as soon as they saw me, they both got up and Alcides walked in with some drinks. The one who wanted to meet with me was Mr. De Carvalho, who introduced himself to me, and the other person was his private driver. We sat down, and Mr. De Carvalho had a long look at me before he said that he had been told of my presence by my aunt Ruth. He told me that the family knew about me and they were trying to get together and find a solution to the problem. Unfortunately, the person who would be dealing with the matter was in Europe, and this was why they hadn't contacted me.

Mr. De Carvalho was interested in my life too, and everything that I have said before I had to repeat all over. He was intrigued by me and certainly admitted that I had my father's looks as we shook hands and he promised to help resolve my case.

And yet the days passed and no word from either my aunt Ruth or Mr. De Carvalho. I remained in the country for that month, and nobody sat down with me to find a solution to the problem that had been existing for a decade.

So I left the country, but not the battle for recognition. For as my father would claim, "A luta continua, vitoria e certa" and this I must do—cling to my father's credo.

Lightning Source UK Ltd.
Milton Keynes UK
UKOW03n0521080514

231313UK00001B/2/P